LIFE WITHOUT JURISDICTION

An investigation by Alabama Exposure and Accountability LLC

This book is published to ensure public access to the factual record of this case and to remove barriers to understanding what occurred.

The research, writing, and publication of this book were funded entirely by volunteer advocates.

This publication reflects the factual record and procedural posture of the case as of January 1, 2026. Because the case remains active, updated editions may be printed as new developments occur.

This work is presented for informational and advocacy purposes only. It is not intended as legal advice.

ISBN: 978-0-9660479-1-2
First publication date: January 1, 2026
Published by Page & Palette

United States of America

This book is dedicated to the Lawrence family.

You never stopped telling the truth even when no one in power would listen. This story is dedicated to your persistence, your dignity, and your refusal to let the system bury someone you love. Your fight is the reason the truth is finally seen.

TABLE OF CONTENTS

HOW AND WHY THIS BOOK WAS WRITTEN

This book is grounded entirely in the public record.

Every factual assertion is supported by trial transcripts, sworn testimony, forensic reports, court filings, and contemporaneous documentation. Where the record is silent, that silence is identified. Where evidence was excluded from the courtroom, those omissions are documented and sourced.

The full evidentiary archive underlying this book is publicly available at www.justiceformurraylawrencejr.com. The archive exists so the material can be reviewed independently by investigative journalists, legal scholars, documentary producers, and any reader willing to examine the case on its merits rather than its outcome.

This case does not exist in isolation. The failures documented here reflect structural weaknesses within Alabama's criminal justice system, and specifically within Baldwin County, where other documented cases have raised similar concerns about disclosure practices, evidentiary handling, attorney performance, and institutional oversight. When critical facts are fragmented, when material information is withheld or minimized, and when corrective mechanisms fail to activate, the consequences extend beyond a single prosecution. They become part of an institutional pattern.

This book is not an argument for sympathy. It is a presentation of facts that were never allowed to stand together in one place. Its purpose is exposure, review, and accountability. The record does not require belief. It requires attention.

PROLOGUE

Before anything in this case took shape, the teenagers who would later be pulled into it were living ordinary lives. They spent time with friends, moved between familiar houses, worked small jobs that paid just enough for gas and the things they needed, and followed the same casual routines that marked most nights in Fairhope. Their connections came from neighborhoods, shared history, and the familiarity that comes from growing up in the same place. They knew each other well enough to borrow a car, make plans at the last minute, or stop by without notice.

Brandon Hastings was part of this circle, along with several others who would later appear in the story. At the time they were simply teenagers, meeting up for food, talking about work, and filling their days with the small concerns that come with young adulthood. Their lives held the same predictability found in most small towns. They trusted that tomorrow would look much like today.

Nothing in their world suggested a break from that rhythm. Nothing hinted at a shift that would redraw every relationship and every memory.

They were young people moving through an ordinary night in Baldwin County, Alabama, unaware that the familiar patterns around them would soon give way to a nightmare none of them could have imagined.

This is where the story begins.

1 THE FINAL HOURS OF NORMAL

It is Spring Break, 2003. Several groups of friends gathered across Fairhope, Lake Forest, Daphne, Foley, and Gulf Shores. They are partying not in the sense of a noun, but as a verb, simply getting together in each other's houses and enjoying casual time on a holiday weekend. These young people are between the ages of eighteen and twenty-two and free-spirited. Recreational drug use exists within these circles, most often marijuana and occasionally cocaine, shared at a low level within familiar groups. Throughout the evening, phone calls move between friends and small groups, making plans, changing plans, or deciding to meet at the beach.

On Friday night, 4/5/2003, nineteen-year-old Brandon Hastings stayed in contact with the friends he spent most of his time with, Frank Wright, Leon Shoots, Renauld Langham, Phillip Barham, and Thomas Hobbs. All had ridden or met with him at the beach earlier that evening and returned before midnight to Foley.

Brandon was a stylish, clean cut, small and slender white kid from a stable family. His pride and joy was a white Acura that he kept meticulously maintained. He wore high end brand name clothing and was known to carry a few hundred dollars in cash most of the time. Brandon worked two jobs, including one at Bebo's Car Wash in Foley, and was financially stable for someone his age. His routines were predictable, and his actions that night fit comfortably within them.

The people around Brandon spent the evening meeting up for food, talking about work, and making last minute plans. Their connections came from neighborhoods, shared history, and the familiarity that comes from growing up in the same place. Nothing about the night felt unusual or urgent.

That evening, Jarius McNeil did not have an active cell phone because he had not paid his bill and relied on payphones and nearby landlines to make calls.

Later that night, Brandon crossed paths with Jarius McNeil, a former acquaintance who had recently returned to the area.

They knew each other before Jarius left for the Army. Their connection did not end when Jarius was stationed away from Fairhope. Even while he was in California, they stayed in touch. Calls were made. Contact was maintained. Whatever form their relationship took, it was not casual and it was not fleeting. It endured time, separation, and change. When Brandon encountered Jarius that night, he was not meeting a stranger. He was reconnecting with someone already woven into his life.

Jarius did not belong to Brandon's primary group of friends. Their social circles rarely overlapped, and they were not known for spending time together. Their contact that night stood apart from the otherwise familiar pattern of Brandon's routines.

Jarius had prior legal trouble and had recently been convicted of counterfeiting. He received a less than honorable discharge from the military and had prior convictions for writing bad checks during his time in service in California. His world did not meaningfully intersect with Brandon's social circle, despite limited contact between the two at different points in time.

As the night moved forward, people came and went from familiar places, crossing paths briefly before returning home. These interactions unfolded without concern and without any indication that the ordinary rhythm of the night was breaking.

By the early morning hours of 4/6/2003, families in Fairhope and Foley began their usual routines.

What remains from these hours comes from ordinary interactions and brief encounters that did not stand out at the time. The details of when and where those moments occurred are accounted for in the timeline that follows.

2 RECORDED TIMELINE OF EVENTS

The hours that follow were, at the time, ordinary. They were the final hours of normal before everything shifted. Over the years, those hours have been retold through testimony, argument, and reconstruction. Rather than narrate what is now known, this section presents the sequence as it was documented then. A structured timeline prevents hindsight from reshaping memory, allowing each call, each sighting, and each recorded movement to stand in its original order, grounded in the record as it existed in real time before conclusions were imposed.

Friday, 04/05/2003

What follows is a reconstructed factual timeline of the night beginning Friday, 04/05/2003, and extending into Saturday, 04/06/2003. The sequence reflects documented phone activity, recorded time markers, and observed interactions. Times are listed exactly when available. Where precise minutes are not documented, the record reflects approximate placement based on consistent accounts. This timeline is presented without interpretation or hindsight.

All times prior to **2:00 am** are recorded in Central Standard Time. At **2:00 am**, Daylight Saving Time went into effect and clocks advanced directly to **3:00 am**, removing one hour from the recorded night. All times thereafter are Central Daylight Time.

Evening hours
During the evening hours of Friday, 04/05/2003, Brandon Hastings spent time with friends in the Gulf Shores and Foley area. Phone activity reflects routine social contact and coordination throughout the evening.
9:46 pm CST

Jarius made a call to Brandon from the Mixson residence landline to meet up later without his friends present.

Between approximately 9:46 pm and midnight
Brandon remained with his friends at the beach earlier and returned to Foley a little after midnight.

Saturday, 04/06/2003

Shortly after midnight
Brandon's phone activity continued at intervals consistent with routine communication.

1:20 am CST
Jarius placed a call to Brandon from a payphone located at the Pick n Pay at the intersection of County Road 12 and County Road 49 to let him know he was close to Foley.

1:30 am CST
Brandon arrived near Bebo's Car Wash in Foley. Debra Fudge, who worked with Brandon at Bebo's, saw him there with Jarius seated in the passenger seat of Brandon's white Acura.

Between approximately 1:30 am and 2:00 am CST
Brandon and Jarius departed the Bebo's area. There are no confirmed sightings of Brandon after this point.

2:00 AM CST
DAYLIGHT SAVING TIME WENT INTO EFFECT CLOCKS ADVANCED DIRECTLY TO 3:00 AM CDT

Between approximately 3:20 am and 3:40 am CDT
Jarius arrived at the Mixson residence in Fairhope. He remained only briefly before leaving. No activity inside the residence was documented during this period.

Early morning hours
Other individuals had been at the residence earlier in the night and had left prior to Jarius's arrival.

Between approximately 4:20 am and 4:45 am CDT
Crystal Lindsey and John Wayne Mixson arrived at the Mixson residence. Their presence was brief before they departed.

5:01 am CDT
A traffic stop involving Crystal Lindsey and John Wayne Mixson occurred in Fairhope. The stop was brief and no arrest was made. The time of the stop was recorded.

As daylight approached
Jarius arrived at the home of Cynthia Weston, his live-in girlfriend, at the time. He arrived as the sun was beginning to rise. Sunrise occurred at approximately **6:30 am CDT**.
This marks the final event in this timeline.

3 THE FIRST DAYS WITHOUT HIM

When the sun rose on Sunday, April sixth, two thousand three, the day began like any other.

Brandon Hastings had not returned home to Foley. At first, that absence did not trigger alarm. He was nineteen. He spent nights with friends. Plans shifted without notice. It was not unusual for him to stay out late or to sleep at someone else's house after a long night.

But as the morning moved forward, calls began.

Friends reached out to one another, asking where he had gone after leaving Bebo's Car Wash. No one had seen him. No one had heard from him. His phone no longer answered.

By midday, uncertainty replaced assumption.

Brandon's white Acura was not at his home. It was not at any friend's residence. The routines that normally explained his movements did not account for his absence.

As Sunday turned into Monday, the concern deepened. Calls were made again. Locations were checked again. The circle of people who had seen him in the early morning hours was retraced. Each conversation produced the same answer. No one knew where he was.

Days passed without contact.

What had begun as a delay became a disappearance.

Search efforts expanded. Information was shared. The last confirmed sightings were revisited. The final phone activity was reviewed. Still, no confirmed trace of Brandon emerged.

Five days after he was last seen, the unanswered questions crossed state lines.

On the morning of 04/11/2003, the Jackson County Sheriff's Department received a call from Donna Ford reporting that she had discovered a human head near the driveway of her residence. Deputies responded and began a search of the surrounding area.

As the search radius expanded, deputies located Brandon Hastings's body along a rough, tree lined path that ended at a small dumpsite. The body was found approximately one hundred yards from where the head had been discovered. The separation occurred at the upper cervical spine. Autopsy findings documented that the first and second cervical vertebrae were missing at that level, and trial testimony later explained that the head separated at the same location where trauma had occurred and where animal activity was evident. Investigators noted that feral dogs were a known problem in the area, and the condition of the remains was consistent with postmortem animal disturbance rather than dismemberment by a person.

The area was remote, overgrown, and difficult to access. The location and condition of the remains suggested they had been intentionally left in a place unlikely to be discovered quickly.

When the body was recovered, the victim's pants were down around his knees and he was not wearing shoes.

The burglary narrative did not align with the condition of the scene. The absence of shoes contrasted with the presence of jewelry on the body. There was no evidence of ransacking, no indication that property had been taken from his person consistent with theft, and no follow through behavior associated with robbery.

Following protocol for unidentified remains, deputies photographed the scene, documented the position and condition of the body, secured the area, and transported the remains to the Jackson County medical examiner.

After the initial recovery and removal of the remains, the coroner returned to the site to conduct a more thorough search of the surrounding area. During that follow up examination, the hyoid bone was located and recovered. The bone was documented and added to the remains for examination.

With the head, body, and hyoid bone now recovered, the Jackson County medical examiner had the components necessary to conduct a full autopsy. The autopsy was conducted in Mississippi, and the cause and manner of death were certified there. The remains were identified as belonging to Brandon Hastings.

Mississippi documented the identification in its official records and issued a death certificate replacing the earlier document that had listed the remains as unidentified. With the identity established, Mississippi authorities were then able to formally notify Brandon's family.

After the identification, the Mississippi coroner contacted Pam Morrison, Brandon's mother, to ask where the remains should be sent. The family requested that Brandon's body be returned home for burial. Mississippi released the remains to Mack Funeral Home for burial only. At that stage, the funeral home's role was strictly custodial and limited to preparation for burial, with no investigative or medical function. Friends, relatives, and members of the community gathered to grieve a young man whose absence had begun only days earlier as worry.

4 WHERE ALABAMA'S VERSION TOOK SHAPE

With Brandon Hastings identified, Mississippi's recovery and forensic process concluded. Responsibility for further investigative action moved to Baldwin County, where authorities began examining the hours before Brandon disappeared. From that point forward, the focus no longer rested on recovery or certification, but on reconstructing events through interviews and statements gathered in Alabama.

While the family mourned, officers continued working on the case. Their focus was to identify Brandon's last contacts and determine where he had been in the hours before he disappeared. Early interviews produced information but did not establish a clear direction.

As investigators compared the statements, most accounts blended into the background. One did not. Jarius McNeil was not part of Brandon's usual circle. His routines and friendships were separate, making his presence with Brandon that night stand out.

When officers reviewed Jarius's statements, they noted repeated changes in his descriptions of where he went after leaving Brandon and how long they remained together. His accounts varied as to the order of locations, the timing of those stops, and whether anyone else was present. In some versions, he placed his separation from Brandon earlier in the night. In others, he extended his timeline later. These discrepancies did not align with phone records or with accounts provided by other witnesses. The inconsistencies remained unresolved, and officers returned to him more than once seeking explanations for the shifting narrative.

During this same period, within weeks of Brandon's death, Jarius was taken into custody on an unrelated charge involving counterfeit currency. He was also charged with possession of stolen property connected to Brandon. His arrest kept him within the Baldwin

County system while investigators continued reconstructing the hours before Brandon disappeared. Because he remained in custody, officers were able to return to him for additional questioning.

Jarius was not unfamiliar with the courthouse environment. His father was a retired United States Marshal, and his mother worked within the Baldwin County court system. He grew up around deputies, investigators, clerks, and judges who knew his family by name. That proximity to federal and local law enforcement distinguished his position from that of the other teenagers involved and formed part of the institutional setting in which his questioning occurred.

According to Debra Fudge, Jarius was the last person seen with Brandon, around 1:30 am in Foley.

5 THE ADMISSION

In the days following 4/6/2003, Jarius was being held in the Baldwin County Jail on charges unrelated to homicide. He had been arrested for counterfeit currency and for possession of property taken from Brandon Hastings's vehicle. While he remained in custody, investigators continued returning to him for questioning.

These sessions did not resemble the earlier interviews.

Officers confronted Jarius with inconsistencies in his prior statements. They told him the case now involved a killing. They warned him that he could face the death penalty. They made clear that cooperation was the only way to avoid it. The warnings were repeated. The pressure was unmistakable.

As the questioning intensified, additional officials entered the room. Their presence marked escalation. The investigative record reflects the involvement of Dean McGowen, an investigator with the Baldwin County District Attorney's Office, and Anthony Lowery, the District Attorney's lead investigator. Both emphasized the consequences Jarius faced. Both pressed him for a complete account. Both reinforced that withholding information would only increase his risk.

The questioning did not stop. Officers asked whether he was telling the whole story. They repeated the threat of capital punishment. They reinforced that cooperation was the only protection available to him.

In the weeks that followed his arrest, the pressure intensified. Officers returned to him repeatedly. They confronted him with inconsistencies. They reminded him that the case involved a homicide and that capital punishment was a possibility. Cooperation was framed as the only protection available to him.

Under that pressure, Jarius admitted that he alone caused Brandon Hastings's death. It was the first admission investigators had obtained that placed responsibility squarely on him without naming anyone else.

On 05/14/2003, approximately five weeks after Brandon was killed, Jarius appeared in court for a bench trial. He waived his right to a jury and proceeded before a judge alone. He did not name an accomplice. He did not describe a second participant. The posture of the case reflected what he had already admitted, that he alone was responsible. No one else was charged. No one else was identified in open court. His sentence remained pending. After his court appearance, investigators removed Jarius from the jail and placed him in a patrol vehicle. Officers drove through Baldwin County while he attempted to identify the location where he claimed the killing had occurred.

He struggled. He examined roads. He changed his mind repeatedly. He asked officers to keep driving.

According to investigative notes consistent with the accounts of Captain Hoss Mack, Dean McGowen, and Anthony Lowery, Jarius spoke hesitantly as they drove. He asked whether they were getting closer. He said certain places looked familiar, then moments later said they were not right. At times he pointed vaguely toward tree lines or side roads, then withdrew those suggestions. He expressed uncertainty about distances and landmarks, questioned whether they had already passed the area, and told officers he needed to see more of the road. His statements shifted as the vehicle moved, offering no stable reference point.

According to those same accounts, Jarius did not point to the same area consistently and appeared confused about the location. After prolonged uncertainty, he eventually settled on a site along Highway 49, a few miles outside Magnolia Springs.

Deputies conducted a full search of the area he indicated and the surrounding terrain. They used dogs, metal detectors, and coordinated ground sweeps. They examined the location thoroughly.

They found no evidence. No blood. No clothing. No disturbed soil. No items belonging to Brandon. Nothing to indicate that a crime had occurred there.

When the search ended, investigators had no physical corroboration, no witness support, and no forensic link to a credible murder site. What they had was a statement made under the threat of capital punishment, followed by a site selection that produced nothing.

Even so, this interrogation marked a turning point.

From that moment forward, the investigation would no longer revolve around what could be proven. It would follow what had been said under pressure.

6 THE REVERSAL

Before Brandon Hastings's body was recovered, an event occurred that would later reshape the case.

On 04/09/2003, Murray Lawrence Sr and his son, Murray Jr, went voluntarily to the Fairhope Police Department. They did so to prevent confusion and to provide information they believed might matter.

That day, a handgun was turned over to police.

Murray Sr explained to Officer Steven Griffis that the gun did not belong to his son. He stated that his godson, Jeff Shaw, had brought the gun to him and said that Jarius had handed it over and asked him to hold my piece. Murray Sr said the weapon was taken into his possession only to secure it. He had no knowledge of any connection between the gun and Brandon's disappearance or death.

At that time, neither Murray Sr nor Murray Jr knew where the gun originated. They did not know who had owned it before Jarius or how it had moved through other hands. Those details emerged later through testimony, not at the moment the gun was surrendered.

The firearm had been reported stolen from John Steadman, a Fairhope resident, on 11/21/2002. It had no connection to Brandon's cause of death. It was a stolen gun Jarius had been attempting to hide while under investigation.

Murray Lawrence Sr turned the gun over voluntarily. Officer Griffis logged it into evidence.

Even with the firearm in evidence, the investigative record did not change. The gun was not subjected to ballistics testing. No forensic analysis was performed. No witness placed anyone else with Brandon. No physical evidence expanded the case beyond Jarius.

On 07/31/2003, while he remained in county jail, Captain Hoss Mack and Dean McGowen questioned Jarius again. By that date, more than two months had passed since his 05/14/2003 bench trial. He had not named an accomplice in court. He had not described a shooting. His sentence was still pending. The death penalty was raised once more.

During this interrogation, officers asked Jarius about the firearm.

What gun? was his response.

Only after that denial did he realize investigators were referring to the stolen Steadman gun. At that point, the dynamic shifted.

This was the moment the story changed.

Jarius moved from admitting that he alone caused Brandon Hastings's death to supplying a new narrative that placed responsibility on someone else.

One hundred sixteen days after admitting sole responsibility and leading investigators on a site visit that produced no confirmed location, investigators returned to him again. He had taken responsibility without naming anyone else. He had participated in a site visit based on that admission. The introduction of a second person as the shooter represented a reversal of his earlier account.

For the first time, he named Murray Lawrence Jr, known to friends as Bubba. For clarity and consistency, this narrative refers to him as Murray Jr.

As part of this revised account, Jarius stated that earlier that night he told Brandon a friend needed help with a vehicle that had broken down. According to this version, that request explained why Brandon would leave his usual routine.

Jarius described a scenario in which Brandon's car was pulled off the side of the road on a downward slope. Brandon stood on one side of the vehicle while Jarius remained nearby. The hood was raised. Jarius claimed that Murray Jr approached from the opposite side, stepped forward, extended his arm, pointed the handgun, and fired across the width of the car.

The distance described, measured across the vehicle, would have been approximately six and a half to seven feet.

Jarius offered no motive for the killing. He described no argument, threat, or conflict that would explain why Murray Jr would have committed such an act. He stated that he lured Brandon to the location by saying a friend had car trouble, which explained why the hood was raised. He did not explain why he himself would have been present but uninvolved, or how the events he described resulted in Brandon's death.

There is no indication in the investigation record that this reversal was challenged.

There is no documented effort to reconcile the new firearm story with the earlier admission, no explanation for why the original account was abandoned, and no testing of plausibility.

Instead, the revised narrative was accepted.

On 08/01/2003, investigators conducted another road trip. This occurred days after Jarius's reversal. The record does not establish whether this trip returned to the same location previously searched or to a different area. No physical evidence was recovered.

Notably, Jarius's original admission did not include a firearm. He did not describe a shooting. He did not introduce a weapon. He did not name an accomplice. That admission was followed by a site visit that produced no evidence.

From that point forward, the investigation no longer centered on what Jarius had admitted doing alone. It followed the narrative built around the gun.

At the time of the investigation, information later obtained through interviews reflected that Jarius was not open about his sexual orientation with friends or family. Those same interviews confirmed that his father was a retired United States Marshal. The record contains no direct evidence that his father intervened, requested protection, or influenced decisions.

What the record shows is a complete reversal of Jarius's account without the introduction of new physical evidence. The record does not explain why investigators accepted that change without challenge.

7 WHAT IT TOOK TO MAKE IT STICK

After the revised account was accepted as fact, the investigation shifted away from examining whether the story was true. The focus turned to making the story work.

Statements taken in the days immediately following April 6, 2003, did not place Murray Jr near Brandon Hastings, Jarius, or the events of that night. Those early accounts were clear and consistent.

What followed was not the discovery of new facts, but a process of revisiting old ones. Once investigators committed to a theory, later interviews took on a different function. They were no longer aimed at determining what happened, but at ensuring that nothing contradicted what now had to be sustained.

Investigators returned to witnesses they had already interviewed, not to clarify facts, but to apply pressure. Over the course of the investigation, at least seventeen individuals, including civilian witnesses, investigators, and one police officer, were subjected to threats, intimidation, leverage, silence, incentive, or sustained interrogation. Not all altered their accounts. Some resisted. Others withdrew. Most accounts shifted in timing, emphasis, or implication under this pressure. What changed universally was the environment in which statements were produced.

The pattern repeated.
A clear first statement.
A return visit.
A threat, deal, or silence.
A revision, withdrawal, or softening.

Cynthia Weston, who had been in an on again off again relationship with Jarius, gave a direct account in her first statement. She stated that Jarius arrived at her home alone in the early morning hours of

April 6. He acted distant and insisted on sitting in the dark. He left shortly after arriving. She placed no one with him and did not mention Murray Jr. When investigators returned, the tone changed. She was warned she might be protecting Jarius and told she could face consequences. Her certainty softened, not because her memory changed, but because the risk did.

Blair Gordon, who knew Brandon Hastings and his family, stated in her earliest account that she had not seen Murray Jr with Brandon and had not seen him at all that night. Nothing in her statement supported the direction the investigation would later take. When she was brought back in, she was told her account did not add up and warned she could face charges. Subsequent interviews introduced uncertainty and vague references to guns and violence that had never appeared before.

Crystal Curtis Lindsey initially described only her own movements. She placed herself and John Wayne Mixson with Murray Jr around 4:45 a.m. and described being stopped by police at 5:01 a.m. in Fairhope. Her account placed him in Fairhope, not Mississippi. When investigators returned, she was told she could be treated as an accessory if she did not help herself. She did not change her original account.

John Wayne Mixson, already dealing with unrelated legal trouble, stated in his initial interview that he saw Murray Jr inside the Mixson residence wearing pajama bottoms at approximately 4:45 a.m. He did not place him with Brandon Hastings or at the events surrounding Brandon's disappearance. When investigators returned, they leveraged Mixson's legal exposure and made clear that cooperation could affect his own situation. As the pressure escalated, Mixson's attorney, John Beck, advised him to invoke the Fifth Amendment, and he declined to answer further questions.

Stacey Giambrone initially stated that she was at Tonya Mixson's house and saw Murray Jr there, leaving around 2:30 a.m., or 3:30

a.m. daylight saving time. She never recanted the fact that she saw him. When investigators returned, she was warned she could be charged and told she might go down with them. Her later statements reflected fear rather than memory.

Damien Heard, Jarius's half-brother, described only his own involvement with the stripped Acura in his initial statement. Murray Jr did not appear in his account. Under repeated questioning and threats of serious charges, Damien's later statements shifted to place his own actions closer in time and proximity to Murray Jr, without adding any firsthand observation of violence or involvement in Brandon Hastings's death. His fingerprint was the only one found on the stripped vehicle. He was in Panama City, Florida, on spring break on April 4 and 5, returning late on April 6. His statements changed. The underlying facts did not.

Tonya Mixson initially stated that she and Murray Jr were asleep together in bed at her Fairhope residence when Jarius arrived during the early morning hours, around 2:30 a.m., or 3:30 a.m. daylight saving time, after Stacey left. She said they both woke when Jarius tapped on the window. Tonya looked out while Murray Jr went outside to speak with him. At that time, car speakers had already been placed on the porch, and neither Tonya nor Murray Jr recognized the vehicle Jarius was driving. After the brief exchange, Jarius left, and Tonya and Murray Jr returned to bed. Later that morning, between approximately 4:30 and 4:45 a.m., they were awakened again when John Wayne Mixson and Crystal Curtis Lindsey arrived seeking cocaine. Tonya was interviewed repeatedly, more extensively than any other witness. During questioning, investigators raised the possibility of drug related charges, stolen property, and hindering prosecution. No female investigators were present. In later statements, her account shifted from certainty to uncertainty.

Elizabeth Mixson initially stated that Jarius came to the residence earlier in the evening, around 9:30 p.m., and that Murray Jr was not present. She went to bed around 10:30 p.m. and did not witness later events. After repeated questioning, her statements shifted in tone and structure, reflecting investigator phrasing rather than her own observations.

Michelle Heard later turned over jumper cables to investigators. The cables were entered into evidence and labeled as associated with a suspect. The record does not show that the cables were forensically tested, and no blood, DNA, or trace evidence was identified. Despite this, the cables were referenced narratively to imply a physical mechanism, even though no murder weapon was recovered and the method of death was strangulation.

Brooks Miller was not contacted in the immediate aftermath of Brandon Hastings's death. According to Brooks, investigators first reached out after the State's theory had already taken shape. She had no relationship with Jarius, no knowledge of the crime, and no information tying Murray Jr to Brandon Hastings or to any act of violence. Investigators initially asked her to come in to talk. When she rescheduled, they treated the delay as suspicious. She was then formally subpoenaed and traveled from Louisiana, only to be told she was not needed. Her involvement ended once it became clear she could not advance the narrative.

Steve Heard's testimony was limited to what he overheard. He stated only that he heard Jarius speaking on the phone with Damien Heard about trying to sell a gun. He did not see a gun. He did not witness any act of violence. He did not place Murray Jr at a scene of violence or describe him handling a firearm. Despite those limits, his account was repeatedly pressed beyond what he personally observed, shifting the focus of his testimony toward a firearm narrative that he could not independently support.

Frank Wright's initial statements did not place Murray Jr with Brandon Hastings or at the scene of the homicide. His account did not support the State's emerging theory. Investigators nonetheless returned to Wright multiple times after the narrative had shifted, questioning him about motive and associations rather than events he claimed to have witnessed. Wright did not provide testimony tying Murray Jr to the crime, but his repeated reinterviews reflect the same investigative pattern.

Michael Dozier's earliest statements did not place Murray Jr at the scene of the homicide or describe him participating in violence. As the investigation progressed, Dozier was questioned again under the threat of a drug related investigation and was pressured to support a motive driven narrative rather than a factual account of events. Despite that pressure, Dozier consistently confirmed that he was with Murray Jr at the Mixson residence at approximately 1:00 a.m. on April 6, 2003, a detail that contradicted the State's theory and remained unchanged.

Jeff Shaw's account never changed. He stated consistently that Jarius left a firearm with him to hold. He explained that he later gave that gun to Murray Sr and Murray Jr only so it could be turned over voluntarily to police. Shaw did not describe Murray Jr as owning the gun, possessing it independently, or using it in any way. He did not connect him to violence or to the homicide. Shaw was the last known custodian of the Steadman gun before it was surrendered, and his testimony established that fact clearly.

Despite this, the prosecution reframed Shaw's words. Ownership and significance were shifted onto Murray Jr, even though Shaw's account did not support that narrative.

Steve Griffis accepted the firearm voluntarily turned in by Murray Sr and Murray Jr as part of an unrelated stolen property matter. In later reports, Griffis altered that account, reframing the same firearm as the murder weapon. That shift occurred without forensic support and contrary to the medical findings.

Anthony Lowery, an investigator for the District Attorney, was centrally involved in the repeated interrogations that followed the adoption of the State's theory. He participated in multiple interviews with key witnesses as statements were revisited and revised. These interrogations intensified over time and coincided with moments when prior accounts were softened, narrowed, or altered. Lowery's involvement placed him at the center of the process through which witness testimony evolved without the discovery of new physical or forensic evidence.

Captain Hoss Mack supervised and participated in interrogations during the critical phase of the investigation when the death penalty was raised and Jarius's account changed. These sessions coincided with a shift in the prosecution's theory, despite no corresponding discovery of physical or forensic evidence. Mack later oversaw investigative efforts tied to those statements that yielded no corroboration.

Jarius initially admitted that he alone caused Brandon Hastings's death. Only after renewed threats of capital punishment did he accuse Murray Jr.

By the time the State's theory hardened, the record already carried a pattern that could not be ignored. The same names appeared repeatedly across interviews, follow up visits, revised statements, warnings, threats, and deals. Each time the investigation stalled, pressure returned to the same people. Most of them were very young adults at the time.

At least seventeen individuals were subjected to this process, excluding Brooks Miller, who was included for full context.

They were:

Cynthia Weston

Blair Gordon

Crystal Curtis Lindsey

John Wayne Mixson

Stacey Giambrone

Damien Heard

Tonya Mixson

Elizabeth Mixson

Michelle Heard

Steve Heard

Frank Wright

Michael Dozier

Jeff Shaw

Steve Griffis

Anthony Lowery

Captain Hoss Mack

Jarius McNeil

Not one of these individuals ever provided a firsthand account placing Murray Jr at the scene of the murder or describing him committing an act of violence. Even after pressure. Even after threats. Even after incentives. The State could not produce a single eyewitness to the crime itself. Every altered statement moved in the same direction. None supplied the missing proof.

The number matters.
The repetition matters.
The uniformity matters.

Every shift occurred only after Jarius, under threat of the death penalty, moved from admitting he acted alone to accusing an innocent man. Those shifts did not arise from newly discovered facts. They followed original statements that were already complete, contemporaneous, and unambiguous. Rather than proceed on the record they had, investigators chose to revisit witnesses they had already interviewed, returning to the same individuals repeatedly in an effort to force the narrative to fit. It took eleven months to accomplish that effort. Investigators did not uncover a conspiracy. They sustained one by leaning on fear, vulnerability, and the promise that cooperation meant safety while resistance carried consequences.

The question is why an investigation that claimed to be grounded in truth required at least seventeen pressured voices, most of them very young adults, to survive at all.

8 THE UNAVOIDABLE ARREST

By June 3, 2004, nearly eleven months had passed since Brandon Hastings was killed and since Jarius confessed to the murder. During that time, investigators revisited witnesses, reworked timelines, and expanded the case repeatedly. Only after that extended effort was Murray Jr arrested at his job at the Grand Hotel.

After the firearm narrative took hold, no physical evidence connected Murray Jr to Brandon Hastings's death. There was no DNA, no fingerprints, no blood, no fibers, no ballistics, no gunshot residue, and no established crime scene. No eyewitness ever placed him at the scene or described him committing an act of violence. Murray Jr had no criminal record. The only offense on his record was a traffic citation.

What investigators did have was a story.

That story came from a man who had already admitted that he alone caused Brandon's death. A man who had changed his account under the renewed threat of the death penalty. A man who had failed to lead investigators to evidence. A man whose version of events had already shifted. A man the prosecutor would later acknowledge in court was a liar.

Still, the case moved forward.

By June of 2004, the absence of proof was no longer treated as a problem to be solved. It had become something to be worked around.

The arrest did not rest on forensic proof. It did not rest on eyewitness testimony. It did not rest on physical evidence of any kind. It rested entirely on the word of the admitted killer.

A killer who had first said he acted alone. A killer who had later changed his story. A killer whose account could not be reconciled with the physical record or with his own earlier confession.

There is no moment in the record where investigators paused to reconcile those contradictions. No moment where the lack of corroboration halted the process. No moment where the consequences of being wrong were weighed against the convenience of proceeding.

An accusation made under pressure was carried for almost a year, sustained by coercion and repetition, until it hardened into certainty. By the time Murray Jr was taken into custody, the question was no longer whether the evidence supported the arrest.

The arrest itself had become the evidence.

And that is how a case with no physical proof, no eyewitness, no forensic foundation, and no consistent narrative was taken all the way from an interrogation room to a set of handcuffs. Not because the truth had been found, but because the story had been chosen.

9 THE COURTROOM OPENS

The trial of Murray Jr opened inside the Baldwin County courthouse under Judge Robert Earl Wilters. Prospective jurors were ushered into the courtroom and directed to their seats by court staff. The setting was formal and tightly controlled. Judge Wilters set the tone immediately through his opening instructions to the jury.

Members of the Lawrence family sat toward the back of the courtroom. When Murray Sr attempted to move closer for a clearer view, courtroom staff spoke to him sharply and directed him away. The transcript does not preserve their exact words, but the exchange was described as abrupt and dismissive. Before testimony began, the imbalance toward the family was already visible.

Murray Jr entered the courtroom with his attorney, Wilmer "Willie" E Huntley, who had been privately retained by the Lawrence family. Huntley carried no visible materials suggesting an organized defense strategy. Before any testimony was heard, he gave Murray Jr two specific instructions that would shape both how the jury perceived him and how Murray Jr experienced his own trial.

When Murray Jr asked Huntley whether he should cut his hair, Huntley told him no. He said the longer hair made him look younger. As a result, after weeks in jail without grooming, Murray Jr appeared before the jury with a full afro.

Huntley then instructed Murray Jr to put on a pair of headphones connected to a laptop Huntley had brought into the courtroom. These were not assistive listening devices. Once Murray Jr put them on, he could no longer hear the courtroom. He could not hear the questions, the testimony, or the exchanges between counsel and the judge. He watched his own trial unfold in silence.

Race was an unmistakable presence in the courtroom. It was known to both sides that Brandon Hastings, the victim, was white and that Murray Jr, the defendant, was Black. It was also known that Murray Jr was living with a white woman at the time. These facts existed within the social context of Baldwin County.

The jury ultimately seated included one black juror; the remaining jurors were white.

Jury selection moved quickly under Judge Wilters's control. Prospective jurors were questioned by District Attorney John David Whetstone and Huntley, though Huntley's participation was limited. Under Alabama law, Huntley had broad authority during jury selection. He could challenge jurors for cause, probe for bias, exercise peremptory strikes, and request further questioning when a response raised concern. He exercised almost none of that authority, engaging only minimally and leaving obvious areas of bias and concern unexplored.

The voir dire record, which is the official transcript of jury selection and juror questioning, reflects expressions of bias that went unchallenged. At least one prospective juror indicated discomfort with interracial relationships. Another expressed uncertainty about their ability to remain fair. The relevance of these statements was direct.

In another instance, a prospective juror disclosed familiarity with law enforcement officers involved in the investigation. Huntley did not question whether that relationship could affect impartiality. Judge Wilters continued to move the process forward, and Huntley made no effort to slow or redirect the questioning. Each irregular response passed without challenge.

When the jury was seated and the judge called for the first witness, Murray Jr remained at the counsel table wearing headphones. He used them intermittently during trial, including at moments when testimony was being offered. During those periods, he could not hear what was being said against him. Huntley did not pause the proceedings to ensure Murray Jr could hear the testimony, did not relay what was being said, and did not request any accommodation that would allow his client to fully hear or participate in his own trial.

To the jury, Murray Jr appeared quiet and passive beside his attorney, unaware that he had been placed in enforced silence.

From the outset, the posture of the case was clear. Judge Wilters controlled the courtroom, and District Attorney Whetstone advanced a polished, unified narrative. The few objections Huntley raised were quickly overruled. Murray Jr's own attorney had given him instructions that shaped both his appearance and, at times, his ability to hear the proceedings against him. From the back of the courtroom, his father watched, still unsettled by how he had been addressed only moments earlier.

The trial began under these conditions.

.

10 TWO THEORIES, NO EVIDENCE

The State proceeded under a charge of capital murder, a designation that under Alabama law carries only two possible punishments: death or life without the possibility of parole. That classification governed how the case was presented, the stakes attached to each witness's testimony, and the framework within which the jury was asked to evaluate the evidence. It defined the legal posture of the trial before any testimony was heard.

The State opened its case by calling Dr Paul McGarry, the Mississippi forensic pathologist who performed the autopsy on the remains of Brandon Hastings. His qualifications were established methodically for the jury. By the time questioning turned to the autopsy itself, it was clear that McGarry was the medical authority on the cause of death.

During questioning, District Attorney John David Whetstone framed the death as a violent attack, using language that gestured toward the involvement of a firearm. His questions assumed mechanisms of injury beyond strangulation and invited the jury to consider scenarios not supported by the medical record.

"Is it possible," Whetstone asked, "for certain injuries to mask other forms of trauma, including injuries caused by a gunshot?"

McGarry stated his findings plainly. Brandon Hastings died from asphyxiation due to ligature strangulation. The examination revealed soft tissue injury to the neck and internal indicators consistent with asphyxia.

"The cause of death was ligature strangulation," McGarry testified. "There was no gunshot wound," McGarry stated. "There was no firearm injury."

Mississippi maintained custody of the body from recovery through examination, and the autopsy findings were documented in the official death certificate.

At no point did McGarry alter or soften his conclusion. The cause of death was not in dispute within the medical findings.

Any ambiguity entered only through questioning.

Whetstone began introducing hypothetical scenarios that did not arise from the facts of this case. He referenced rare circumstances in which certain marks might resemble other forms of trauma and asked whether injuries could sometimes be misinterpreted, even when those circumstances were not present here. Each time, McGarry corrected the premise. He reiterated that there was no gunshot injury, no projectile, and no indication of firearm involvement. Despite these answers, the questioning continued in a manner that suggested uncertainty, creating the impression of doubt where none existed in the medical record.

As the questioning pressed forward, Whetstone emphasized what had not been found. No rope. No cord. No identifiable ligature recovered from the scene or from the body. That absence was not presented as a limitation of the investigation, but as a way to cast doubt on the clarity of the medical conclusion.

Yet the absence of a recovered ligature did not undermine the cause of death and did not advance a firearm theory. Strangulation does not require the recovery of the instrument used, and the medical findings did not depend on the presence of a rope or cord.

That complication was reinforced when physical objects unrelated to the autopsy findings were introduced.

Jumper cables were later entered into evidence after being turned over by Michelle Heard. No forensic testing connected the cables to Brandon Hastings. No blood, DNA, or trace evidence was identified. No witness placed the cables at the scene. No expert testified that they were used on the victim or were consistent with the injuries described in the autopsy.

The cables served a visual function rather than an evidentiary one.

They substituted for a missing ligature without committing the State to a specific mechanism. At the same time, they preserved the option of a firearm based narrative, keeping both theories alive despite neither being supported by physical evidence tying them together.

The effect was not to explain how Brandon Hastings was killed, when it occurred, or by whom. It was to avoid answering those questions.

Defense attorney Willie Huntley had the opportunity to address the clarity of the Mississippi findings through cross examination. He did not ask McGarry to restate the cause of death or to read directly from the death certificate. His cross examination was brief, and the forensic findings, while clear in the record, were left without reinforcement before the jury.

Before trial, Captain Hoss Mack had expressed reluctance about calling McGarry to testify, according to investigative notes and internal discussions reflected in the record, stating that the documentation was sufficient. Despite that position, the testimony proceeded, and the clarity of the medical findings was gradually overshadowed by implication rather than evidence.

With the forensic anchor weakened, the State shifted its focus.

The firearm was brought into view of the jury and framed through questioning as significant. The prosecution referred to it as "the gun in question" and, at one point, as "the murder weapon," a phrase preserved in the transcript. That framing suggested relevance not supported by the autopsy findings, and no acknowledgment was made that firearm injury had been excluded by the medical examiner.

As the State's case neared its conclusion, the absence of evidence could no longer be disguised by implication alone.

Defense counsel cross examined Officer Anthony Fuqua of the Foley Police Department, one of the investigators involved in tracking Brandon Hastings's vehicle and the recovery of items later characterized as stolen property, and who attended the autopsy in Mississippi. The exchange was brief.

Huntley asked whether Fuqua had any fingerprints belonging to Murray Jr.
Fuqua answered that he did not.

Huntley asked whether Fuqua had recovered any stolen property from Murray Jr.
Fuqua answered that he had not.

Huntley asked whether Fuqua knew of any stolen property ever traced back to Murray Jr.
Fuqua answered that he did not.

Huntley asked whether Fuqua had been told that Murray Jr was the last person seen with Brandon Hastings.
Fuqua answered that he had not.

Huntley asked whether Fuqua had any fingerprints tying Murray Jr to Brandon Hastings's vehicle.
Fuqua answered that he did not.

Huntley asked whether any weapon had been recovered from Murray Jr.
Fuqua answered that none had.

Huntley asked whether any cell phone records connected Murray Jr to Brandon Hastings.
Fuqua answered that they did not.

The testimony established that law enforcement had recovered no physical evidence, no stolen property, no forensic material, and no documentary link connecting Murray Jr to the homicide. Officer Fuqua was relieved of investigative duties partway through the case. The record does not state why.

A forensic examiner testified that no blood was found on the gun. Huntley challenged the chain of custody and raised questions about the firearm's handling, but those objections were overruled. The absence of blood was not developed for the jury, and the firearm was never squarely framed as unrelated to the cause of death, despite the medical findings and the lack of forensic connection.

The State advanced its narrative through leading questions, selective emphasis, and implication. Hypotheticals replaced conclusions. The autopsy findings were pushed to the margins through suggestion rather than contradiction.

The testimony established the medical facts of Brandon Hastings's death. Strangulation was identified as the cause. No gunshot wound was found. No firearm injury was documented.

The prosecution never committed to a single evidence-based explanation of how Brandon Hastings was killed. Instead, it advanced overlapping narratives, strangulation without a ligature and a firearm without a gunshot wound. Objects were introduced to suggest mechanisms that could not be reconciled with the medical findings. The effect was not to clarify the evidence but to muddy it, allowing the case to proceed without resolving the contradictions at its core.

11 LEADING THE KILLER'S TESTIMONY

Jarius took the stand as the admitted killer of Brandon Hastings and the State's central witness, but he testified as if he were an accomplice rather than the person who had originally confessed to acting alone. By the time he testified, he had already changed his story multiple times, denied involvement, admitted to lying to police, and faced the death penalty before agreeing to cooperate. The jury did not hear those shifts as a sequence. They heard a single version, delivered through a tightly controlled examination.

From the opening question, the structure of Jarius's testimony was supplied by the prosecution. The questions did not ask what happened. They told the jury what had happened and required Jarius only to agree.

Whetstone asked, "Was there any prearrangement that you had with Bubba (Murray Jr) about notifying each other about where each other was so you could set up the luring of Brandon Hastings?" Jarius answered, "Yes," then followed the premise already embedded in the question. The plan, the coordination, and the intent were assumed before the answer was given.

Whetstone continued by walking Jarius step by step through a detailed narrative of planning, location, timing, and intent. He asked whether Murray Jr knew the road. Jarius answered, "Yes, sir." He asked whether that road was isolated in the early morning hours. Jarius answered, "Yes, sir." Each answer accepted the framing without the jury being told that Jarius had never described such a plan before facing capital murder.

When Whetstone asked, "So Bubba (Murray Jr) knew the plan was to pretend that his car was disabled?" Jarius again answered, "Yes, sir." No objection was raised to the leading nature of the question. The plan was not described by the witness. It was supplied to him.

As the testimony progressed, Jarius adopted the prosecution's language. He testified that Murray Jr pulled out a gun and shot Brandon Hastings. Jarius claimed three different times that the shot struck Brandon in the head area, a statement that directly conflicted with the medical findings the jury had already heard.

Whetstone reinforced the narrative by repeating details and prompting agreement. "He was hit in the head, one shot." Jarius responded, "Yes, sir." "The kid never had a chance, did he?" Jarius answered, "No, sir." These were conclusions, not observations, and they were supplied by the questioner.

Throughout this testimony, Jarius acknowledged that he had lied repeatedly to police in earlier statements. He admitted that he denied involvement, denied knowing what happened to Brandon Hastings, and denied causing his disappearance. He admitted those statements were lies. He further admitted that he did not begin telling this version of events until after he was charged with capital murder and understood he was facing the death penalty.

During the State's presentation of its case, District Attorney John David Whetstone addressed the jury directly and explained the State's reliance on Jarius:

"And Jarius, young man as well, a man who I have made a deal with, a deal with the devil so that evidence could be heard, so the dots could be connected. If you don't like that deal, you come after your D.A. I made the decision. I didn't make it lightly, but I made it."

On cross examination, defense counsel confirmed that Jarius would no longer face execution and that he would receive a life sentence with the possibility of parole. Jarius acknowledged that he was testifying under that agreement. The jury heard that exchange, but it was not tied back to the manner in which his testimony had been constructed on direct examination.

What was not done on cross examination mattered more than what was. Defense counsel did not walk the jury through the sequence of Jarius's statements, did not place his prior admissions of sole responsibility side by side with his trial testimony, and did not force reconciliation between his original confession and the version offered after the threat of execution. The jury was told that Jarius had lied before, but it was never shown how his story changed, when it changed, or what pressure coincided with those changes.

Without that context, the jury was left with a false sense of stability. The testimony appeared consistent because its evolution was never exposed. What should have been the central credibility issue of the case was reduced to a single acknowledgement that Jarius had lied in the past, untethered from the reason he was now telling a different story.

Later, defense counsel returned to the language the prosecution itself had used:

"I don't want you to hear it from me. I wanted you to hear the words from the liar, the manipulator, the devil. The District Attorney called him the devil. Did you hear his words? Do you remember that?"

What the jury heard was not a spontaneous confession. It was testimony built through supplied premises, guided answers, and unchallenged conclusions. It came from the admitted killer, after repeated lies, and after the threat of execution. The jury was never asked to account for that.

12 WHAT THE JURY HEARD

After the State presented the testimony of Jarius, the trial moved fully away from forensic evidence and into narrative witnesses. From that point forward, the case against Murray Jr was built almost entirely through testimony rather than physical proof.

In the earliest days of the investigation, none of the witnesses who later testified had placed Murray Jr with Brandon Hastings or described him committing any act of violence. At trial, the jury was not shown those early statements or when Murray Jr's name first entered the narrative. Instead, witnesses appeared in a sequence that presented the accusation as settled rather than developed.

Defense counsel cross examined witnesses individually, but he did not confront them with prior inconsistent statements, did not reconcile early accounts with later testimony, and did not object when questioning moved beyond firsthand knowledge. The jury heard testimony, but not how that testimony evolved.

As the testimony shifted away from forensics, the State introduced character related references. Through witness order and emphasis, Murray Jr was portrayed as connected to drug activity and criminal associations. References were made to drug use, access to drugs, and proximity to people involved in drugs. No witness testified that Murray Jr sold drugs to Brandon Hastings, met Brandon for a drug transaction, or engaged in drug activity with him on the night of the homicide.

Michael Dozier testified about drug use and access to a vehicle on the night before the murder. He did not witness violence, did not see a weapon, and did not place Murray Jr with Brandon Hastings. He did confirm being with Murray Jr at the Mixson residence at 1:00 am.

Andrew Dios, a T Mobile employee, authenticated historical cell tower records and testified that a one twenty am call from Brandon Hastings's phone connected to a tower serving the Pick n Pay area on County Road forty nine. Rusty Willis, a GulfTel employee, testified about the existence and operation of the pay phone at that location and confirmed the call attempts made from it, including the call placed by Jarius. Neither witness testified that Murray Jr made or received a call, was present at the pay phone, or coordinated with Jarius.

Blair Gordon, who knew Brandon Hastings from school and was the only witness who also knew his family, testified that Murray Jr had spoken about a gun and about killing someone. Under questioning by the prosecutor, she said Murray Jr was "going to shoot it," that it would be "the next night," and that he wanted to "kill somebody." She clarified that the conversation occurred on April 4, the night before Brandon Hastings was killed, not the night of the homicide. No other witness corroborated her account, and no forensic evidence supported it.

Damien Heard testified under a grant of immunity after being arrested for receiving stolen property connected to the stripped Acura. His fingerprints were the only ones found on the vehicle. At trial, he did not testify that Murray Jr committed the murder or that he witnessed any violence. He relayed statements suggesting Murray Jr "might have had" speakers or was "supposed to help hide stuff," while admitting he did not see Murray Jr take any property and had no firsthand knowledge of his involvement.

Michelle Heard testified that she voluntarily surrendered jumper cables later referenced by the State. The cables were not forensically tested and produced no evidentiary results.

Steve Heard testified about an overheard phone conversation between Damien Heard and Jarius involving the sale of a stolen toolbox and mention of a gun. He admitted he never saw a gun, could not identify its caliber, and confirmed that Murray Jr was not part of the conversation.

Lieutenant Steve Griffis testified that Mr Lawrence had said he "believed he could put his hands on the weapon that killed that boy that was dumped in Mississippi." Griffis attributed that statement to Mr Lawrence. The record shows that the firearm was voluntarily surrendered by Murray Sr and Murray Jr on April 9, 2003. Brandon Hastings's body was not discovered in Mississippi until April 11, 2003.

Dr Kenneth Mattox testified after viewing the body following the Mississippi autopsy. He did not alter the cause of death and testified that the findings identified no evidence of a gunshot wound.

Dean McGowen testified that during interrogation Jarius changed his story and began implicating Murray Jr. He did not testify about earlier admissions, when Murray Jr's name first appeared, or the circumstances surrounding the change.

Murray Lawrence Sr was called by the State and questioned at length about his actions surrounding the voluntary surrender of the firearm. His testimony established that he and his son went together to retrieve the gun from Jeff Shaw and turned it over to law enforcement at the request of police. He stated that the gun was empty, that he did not handle it, and that he acted out of concern for doing the right thing.

The questioning then turned to Murray Sr's character and reputation. Questions suggested criminal associations, drug involvement, and prior knowledge of guilt. No forensic proof, eyewitness testimony, or evidence tied those implications to the charged offense.

The following exchange reflects questions posed by the prosecutor and answers given by Murray Sr during cross examination.

Q Have you ever told your son that you were a member of a street gang known as The Bloods
A No I haven't

Q Do you have any reason why he would tell his girlfriend that you were a member of a street gang known as The Bloods
A Street gang

Q Street gang You know who The Bloods are don't you
A They don't have Bloods in Fairhope do they I heard of gangs yeah You hear that on TV all the time

Q You know what Bloods means don't you Mr Lawrence People talk about The Bloods You've never heard that them
A Yeah

Q What does it mean to you
A It's a street gang That's all I know

Q And would you know any reason why your son would tell his girlfriend that you were a member of a street gang known as The Bloods
A I don't believe that

Q Had you heard rumors that he sells cocaine
A No I didn't

Q That's news to you
A Very much so Are you talking about Jarius

Q I'm talking about Bubba Is it news to you that Bubba sells cocaine
A Very much news I never knew that Don't believe it

Q You wouldn't believe that
A No

Q And you wouldn't believe he would shoot somebody either would you
A You probably would but I don't

Q I believe he sells cocaine
A Well

TRANSCRIPT RECORD NOTE
The transcript as provided contains a pagination defect. Page 1255 is missing from the sequence. Page 1254 flows directly to page 1256 without certification note, recess notation, or explanation.

By the end of the testimony phase, the jury had heard a collection of statements, implications, and technical facts arranged to read as one story. The pieces appeared to fit. The jury was asked to accept the arrangement as truth.

13 THE GUN AND HOW IT ENTERED THE RECORD

By the time the jury reached deliberations, the State had chosen to center its case on a firearm. The gun was no longer peripheral. It had become the mechanism through which the prosecution attempted to explain the death of Brandon Hastings and assign responsibility to Murray Jr.

That choice mattered because it required the jury to accept a specific sequence of physical events.

The Mississippi autopsy did not identify a gunshot injury. No projectile was recovered. No ballistic evidence tied any firearm to Brandon's death. The medical examiner did not report a gunshot wound, an entry wound, or trauma consistent with a bullet passing through the body. The cause of death was listed as strangulation. The hyoid bone was documented as broken, consistent with strangulation. A gunshot to the neck would be expected to produce gunshot trauma and related ballistic findings, none of which were identified in the autopsy. There was no firearm injury of any kind.

The prosecution's firearm theory rested primarily on testimony. The gun's movement was described through witnesses who placed it with Jarius. No witness placed it in Murray Jr's hands at the time Brandon was last seen alive. That framework had already been laid before the jury.

What had not been laid before them was whether the gun story could physically exist.

As the trial progressed, the State escalated its reliance on the gun narrative. Jarius testified that Murray Jr shot Brandon Hastings in the head area. He further claimed that Brandon's body was then loaded headfirst into the trunk of the Acura.

That testimony required a series of unavoidable physical consequences.

A gunshot wound to the head produces immediate and substantial blood loss. Blood would be present on the victim, on the person handling the body, and throughout the interior surfaces of a trunk if the body were loaded headfirst. Trunk carpeting, padding, seams, and liners retain biological material. There is no realistic way to prevent transfer. There is no realistic way to remove it completely.

The State attempted to supply physical support for this claim through a trunk liner.

The liner became a recurring subject of testimony, objection, and confusion. The court denied motions to dismiss or declare a mistrial and allowed the State to proceed with presenting liner-related evidence while the jury was not present. During these discussions, defense counsel argued that the State had failed to connect the liner to the crime, while the court permitted the prosecution to continue attempting to do so.

When the jury returned, the liner was presented as evidence.

Mack testified that the liner he received had been collected in Mississippi. He stated that he performed a presumptive test for blood on an area that appeared slightly darker in color, describing it as a possible stain. At other points in his testimony, he stated that he saw no stain that would remotely resemble a bloodstain. The testimony did not reconcile these descriptions.

Mack further testified that there was nothing identifying the liner as coming from Brandon Hastings's Honda Acura. He did not testify that it was labeled, marked, or otherwise traceable to that vehicle. He also testified that the liner was never placed into Brandon's car to determine whether it fit.

Despite testimony that a body would have been lying on top of the liner for an extended period of time if the State's version were true, no blood evidence was identified on the liner.

The Department of Forensic Science later examined the liner. That examination did not disclose the presence of blood.

David White testified that he traveled to Mississippi, retrieved the liner, marked it to preserve evidence, and turned it over to Mack. He further testified that he received information about the liner during a July 31 interview. The record reflected no explanation for the delay between that interview and the liner's appearance in evidence months later.

Throughout this testimony, the jury heard repeated references to the liner without clarity on a single essential question. Was this the liner removed from Brandon Hastings's car? The record did not answer that.

What the jury was not told was that even if it were, the liner contradicted the gun narrative rather than supporting it.

No blood was found. No transfer evidence was present. No pooling. No smearing. No indication of cleanup. Nothing consistent with a neck gunshot followed by transport in a trunk.

The testimony required physical evidence that did not exist.

This contradiction was raised outside the presence of the jury. Defense counsel moved for judgment of acquittal, arguing that the State had failed to connect the gun, the liner, or the testimony to a legally sufficient case. The court denied the motion and allowed the case to proceed.

The jury never heard that exchange.

They were not told that the State's theory required physical evidence the State could not produce. They were not told that the liner did not support the story it was offered to explain. They were not told that even taken at face value, the firearm narrative collapsed under the weight of the medical record and the forensic testing.

By the end of trial, the gun had become the centerpiece of the prosecution's theory despite the absence of ballistic evidence, blood evidence, vehicle transfer evidence, or anatomical support. The contradiction was never reconciled. It was simply carried forward.

The jury was never given a framework to test it.

They were not shown how the testimony fit together in time. They were not shown what the physical evidence would have required if the story were true. They were not shown where the record failed to meet the narrative.

When the jury stood to deliberate, they did so having heard a narrative shaped inside the courtroom, unsupported by science, untested by thorough cross examination, and untethered from the autopsy.

What the jury heard was not the full case.

What they were not given would determine everything that followed.

14 THE CONTEXT THE JURY WAS NOT GIVEN

The jury heard testimony. What they were not given was the context necessary to evaluate it, nor the full factual record itself. Critical evidence was omitted entirely. Other facts were presented without the surrounding information that gave them meaning. Without that complete picture, credibility could not be tested, motive could not be measured, and timelines could not be verified.

Most strikingly, no complete timeline was ever established by investigators or presented to the jury at trial. In a capital murder case that turned on precise timing and included a documented clock change in the early morning hours, the absence of a coherent, tested sequence of events is not a minor oversight. It is indefensible. The jury was asked to assess credibility, intent, and participation without ever being shown how the State's theory was supposed to function in time, because no such sequence was ever built.

The confusion was compounded by the Daylight Saving Time change, which removed an hour from the night in question. That disruption alone required careful reconstruction. Instead, testimony was presented in fragments, disconnected from any verified chronology, leaving jurors to reconcile overlapping accounts without temporal anchors.

A full chronology of recorded actions was not assembled until 2023, when volunteers reconstructed the sequence using trial testimony, court filings, phone records, police reports, and admitted exhibits. That reconstruction placed documented actions in time order for the first time and exposed gaps, contradictions, and impossibilities that were never visible to the jury.

The verdict was reached without access to that structure. What the jury evaluated was not a tested sequence of events, but a narrative assembled without time, without context, and without the discipline that the facts required.

For readers who wish to review that structure in full, the complete factual record appears in the section entitled Complete Chronology of Recorded Actions Surrounding the Murder, located before the Index of People in this book. That section presents the documented timeline in comprehensive form, drawn directly from the record, so the sequence of events can be examined as a unified whole rather than as isolated fragments.

What follows is not a dispute over interpretation, but over access. While the jury was shown testimony that had been reshaped inside the courtroom, it was never given the statements, witnesses, and evidence that would have tested the State's theory at its core. Some information existed but was withheld or obscured. Other evidence and witnesses were never placed before the jury at all. These were not marginal details or cumulative points. They were sources of direct alibi, contemporaneous drug evidence, and unfiltered timelines.

The jury was never told that on 05/14/2003, just weeks after Brandon Hastings's death, Jarius waived his right to a jury and pled guilty at a bench trial, admitting under oath that he alone caused Brandon Hastings's death. That admission occurred before Murray Jr was ever charged, yet it was never presented to the jury.

The jury did hear that Jarius had entered into a plea agreement and avoided the death penalty. They were told he would receive life with the possibility of parole. What they were not given was the full chronology of that plea, the timing of the sworn admission of sole responsibility, and a structured comparison between that admission and his later testimony implicating Murray Jr. Without that side by side presentation, jurors were not equipped to evaluate how and why his account evolved.

Nor was the jury given the contextual information the defense could have used to test Jarius's credibility at the time those statements were made and later altered.

Information obtained years later through interviews reflected that Jarius was not open about his sexual orientation during the investigation, a fact that carried social and personal risk in Baldwin County at the time. The jury was never told that Jarius's father was a retired United States Marshal, a role that carried institutional familiarity and authority within law enforcement circles and would have shaped how interactions with investigators were experienced and understood.

There is no evidence of direct intervention or preferential treatment, and none is asserted here. These circumstances are relevant because they provide context for why questions may not have been asked, why pressure may have been applied unevenly, and why an initial sworn admission of sole responsibility was allowed to disappear from the case without scrutiny.

The jury was never given that context when weighing Jarius's shifting statements or the State's reliance on him as its central witness. Without it, the defense failed to equip jurors to evaluate credibility, pressure, and motive in any meaningful way.

This chapter concerns what was withheld and what was excluded, not what was misunderstood. Unlike the witnesses who testified under pressure, incentive, or framing, the witnesses and evidence that follow were removed from the jury's consideration entirely or stripped of the context necessary to be understood. Their absence altered the evidentiary landscape before deliberations ever began, leaving the jury to evaluate a case that appeared complete only because critical pieces were never allowed into view.

Who Did Not Testify

Two individuals with direct relevance to the investigation never testified before the jury. Their absence was not explained, and the consequences of that absence were never acknowledged.

Debra Fudge did not testify. She was the last known person to see Brandon Hastings alive. At approximately 1:30 am on 04 06 2003, she observed Brandon at Bebo's Car Wash in Foley, seated in the driver's seat of his Acura with Jarius in the passenger seat. Her account placed Jarius with Brandon during the critical time window. It also contradicted the State's later suggestion that Murray Jr was the last person with Brandon. The jury never heard her testimony and was never told why she was absent.

Police Officer Windall Thomas did not testify. He conducted the 5:01 am traffic stop of John Wayne Mixson and Crystal Lindsey. That stop established a fixed timestamp placing Murray Jr in Fairhope during the early morning hours, after Brandon Hastings was last seen alive. The jury never heard that evidence because Officer Thomas was not called.

That absence mattered. Jarius testified that he was already in Mississippi during that same period and that Murray Jr had been with him. Both statements could not be true. Yet neither the prosecution nor the defense ever tested the feasibility of that claim by calculating travel time to and from Mississippi, despite relying on that movement as a central premise of guilt. Without Officer Thomas's testimony and without a timed sequence of events, the jury was never allowed to confront that contradiction.

Context Removed from Witness Testimony

Witness testimony established that Brandon Hastings had been riding with friends earlier in the evening before separating from them. The jury heard that none of those individuals knew Brandon was planning to meet Jarius later that night. That information was presented as an isolated fact.

What the jury was not shown was how that fragment fit into a larger timeline. No complete sequence of Brandon's movements was ever assembled or tested. The jury was not shown when Brandon separated from others, how much time passed before his contact with Jarius, or how those movements aligned with recorded calls, sightings, or fixed timestamps. Without that context, the jury could not evaluate whether the State's theory fit the known record.

The jury was also not given personal context that bore directly on credibility.

Blair Gordon had previously made advances toward Murray Jr, which he rejected. Tonya Mixson, his girlfriend at the time, told him that any involvement with Blair Gordon would end their relationship. That interpersonal context was never disclosed to the jury. Without it, Blair Gordon's testimony was presented without the personal tensions and rejected advances that directly affected credibility and motive.

Witness accounts were presented as neutral recollections rather than statements shaped by relationships, timing, and consequence. The jury was asked to assess credibility without knowing what dynamics existed beneath the surface.

Testimony was not false because of what was said. It became misleading because of what was left out.

Statements That Changed Without Disclosure

Several witnesses testified at trial with accounts that differed materially from their earliest statements. The jury heard the revised versions, but it was never told that those versions were not the originals, nor was it told when or why the changes occurred.

In the initial phase of the investigation, witnesses did not place Murray Jr with Brandon Hastings, did not describe him committing violence, and did not identify him as involved in the homicide. Those early statements reflected uncertainty, limited knowledge, or the absence of Murray Jr altogether. At trial, the same witnesses appeared with testimony that implied proximity, intent, or participation.

The jury was presented with the finished product as if it had always existed in that form.

No witness was confronted side by side with prior statements that contradicted their testimony. No timeline was presented showing when revisions occurred. No explanation was given for why certainty increased over time instead of diminishing as memory faded.

This omission mattered because credibility depends on evolution. Without knowing how testimony changed, the jury could not evaluate whether pressure was applied, whether incentives were offered, or whether accounts converged only after repeated questioning.

The jury heard the end result. They were not given the history of how those statements came to be.

Testimony Shaped by Incentive or Pressure

Several witnesses the jury heard did not testify from a neutral position. Their accounts were shaped by immunity, threat of prosecution, or repeated interrogation, none of which was disclosed to the jury in a way that allowed meaningful evaluation of credibility.

Damien Heard testified only after receiving immunity following his arrest for receiving stolen property connected to the stripped Acura. His fingerprints were the only ones found on the vehicle. In his earliest statements, he identified Jarius as the person directing events. At trial, his testimony shifted toward implication rather than observation. He did not testify that Murray Jr committed the murder or that he witnessed violence. Instead, he relayed vague suggestions that Murray Jr might have had speakers or was supposed to help hide stuff, while admitting he did not see Murray Jr take any property and had no firsthand knowledge of his involvement. The jury was not told that this shift followed immunity or that his original account excluded Murray Jr entirely.

Blair Gordon testified that Murray Jr spoke about a gun and about killing someone. Her account was uncertain as to date, location, and timing, and described a gathering the night before the homicide, not the night Brandon Hastings was killed. The jury was not told that these allegations were absent from her earliest statements, nor that no forensic evidence or corroborating witness supported them. The testimony was presented without disclosure of its late emergence or lack of foundation.

Tonya Mixson testified as Murray Jr's girlfriend and as a witness from the home where Jarius returned after the homicide. In her earliest statements, she told investigators that Murray Jr was at the house and asleep during the critical window and did not leave to meet Brandon Hastings. Over time, and after repeated questioning without counsel and warnings about potential charges related to stolen property, her certainty softened. At trial, the jury heard hesitation, but it was not told about the pressure that preceded it.

Cynthia Weston testified about Jarius's arrival at her home in the early morning hours after the homicide, placing him alone and agitated. Her initial account included a specific arrival time that excluded Murray Jr. As questioning continued, she was pressed toward less precise language. The jury was not told that this pressure corresponded to an effort to weaken a timeline that excluded Murray Jr, nor that her testimony never placed him with Jarius or in Mississippi.

In each instance, the jury heard testimony without being told the circumstances under which it was given. Incentives, threats, immunity, and repeated interrogation were treated as collateral rather than central to credibility. The testimony was presented as independent recollection when it was not.

What the jury evaluated as memory was often compliance.

Evidence and Witnesses Removed from the Jury's Consideration

Beyond testimony shaped by pressure or incentive, entire categories of evidence and witnesses were withheld from the jury altogether. These omissions were not matters of emphasis or trial strategy. They were absences that materially altered what the jury was allowed to evaluate.

John Wayne Mixson did not meaningfully testify before the jury. He was permitted to invoke the Fifth Amendment and was never charged. His invocation prevented examination of his conduct during the early morning hours, foreclosed corroboration of Crystal Lindsey's testimony, and blocked inquiry into the 5:01 am traffic stop that placed Murray Jr in Fairhope during the critical window. The jury was never told why this testimony was unavailable or what it would have shown.

Brooks Miller's role in the case raises unresolved questions the trial record cannot answer. Jarius was indicted and convicted within weeks of the homicide following a sealed grand jury proceeding whose witnesses and testimony remain undisclosed. Miller does not appear at Murray Jr's trial despite her proximity to key events and her later appearance in investigative narratives. No discovery from Jarius's case was produced to the defense. What is clear is that the defense was never permitted to see the evidence the State relied upon when it first secured a conviction.

Other investigative voices were removed before trial without explanation. Investigator Anthony Fuqua, a seasoned officer with firsthand involvement in the case who attended the Mississippi autopsy, testified that he could not identify any physical evidence tying Murray Jr to the homicide. He confirmed the absence of fingerprints, stolen property, forensic linkage, or any material connection between Murray Jr and Brandon Hastings's death.

His testimony reflected a straightforward, evidence driven assessment and documented serious concerns about the lack of proof supporting the prosecution's theory. Despite this, Fuqua was relieved of his role partway through the investigation. The record offers no explanation for his removal. It was not disciplinary, and no deficiency in his performance was cited. The jury was never told of his involvement, his findings, or his reassignment. His removal eliminated from the courtroom an investigator whose conclusions directly conflicted with the State's narrative, allowing that narrative to proceed without contradiction from within its own investigative ranks.

These omissions were not neutral. They removed alternative suspects, direct alibi evidence, contemporaneous timestamps, and early exculpatory statements from the jury's consideration. What remained was a narrowed narrative that appeared complete only because contradictory evidence was never allowed into view.

Defense Abandonment and the Missing Context

None of the missing context reached the jury by accident.

Defense counsel had access to the same materials that exposed these gaps. He possessed original witness statements that differed materially from trial testimony. He knew of immunity agreements, interrogation pressure, and shifting timelines. He was aware of excluded witnesses who could have provided direct alibi evidence, contradicted motive, or anchored events to fixed points in time. He did not present them.

At trial, defense counsel cross examined witnesses individually, but he did not restore prior statements to the record, did not confront witnesses with contradictions, and did not force reconciliation between early accounts and later testimony. When implication replaced proof through sequencing and suggestion, he did not interrupt it. When neutral facts were converted into inference, he did not correct the record. When testimony drifted beyond firsthand knowledge, he did not object in a way that stopped it.

More importantly, defense counsel did not supply the jury with what had been kept out entirely. He did not call witnesses whose testimony would have contradicted the State's theory. He did not introduce contemporaneous evidence that undermined motive. He did not explain why witnesses who could have spoken directly to Murray Jr's whereabouts and conduct were absent. Silence filled the space where context should have been.

This was not strategic restraint. It was abandonment of the jury's only safeguard.

The adversarial process depends on one side presenting what the other omits. In this case, that function collapsed. The jury was left to evaluate testimony without the information necessary to test its reliability, credibility, or completeness.

Context and Evidence Withheld

The jury heard testimony. What they were not given was the context necessary to evaluate it, nor the full factual record itself. Critical evidence was omitted entirely. Other facts were presented without the surrounding information that gave them meaning. Without that complete picture, credibility could not be tested, motive could not be measured, and timelines could not be verified. The verdict was reached without access to material facts that would have altered how the testimony was understood in the first place.

15 A COMPROMISED JURY

What became clear only years later was that the jury itself was not functioning as a neutral body bound by the court's instructions, but was instead affected by jury misconduct, meaning jurors were exposed to outside information, improper discussion, pressure, or influence that violated the rules of a fair trial. The problems did not appear on the surface of the trial record. They emerged through juror conduct, private communications, and postconviction disclosures that revealed how the verdict was actually formed.

A jury made of true peers is not passive. Even when a defense is weak, jurors typically register clear contradictions when those contradictions are concrete, repeated, and grounded in common sense. In this case, the jury heard that the autopsy ruled out a gunshot. They heard the prosecution continue to emphasize a gun. They heard the admitted killer describe a shooting. They heard other testimony that placed the firearm with him rather than with the defendant. These were not subtle legal distinctions. They were plain factual conflicts.

Yet juries do not reason in a vacuum. They reason inside the frame they are given.

That frame is not shaped by testimony alone. It is shaped by instruction, enforcement, and consequence.

Just before deliberation, the jury was instructed that circumstantial evidence must be strong and cogent, and of such character as to convince them beyond a reasonable doubt that the defendant was guilty. They were told that circumstantial evidence could support a conviction only if it excluded reasonable interpretations consistent with innocence. If the evidence was sufficient to show a guilty act by some person other than the defendant, or equally consistent with innocence, they were instructed it would not be sufficient to convict.

Those instructions were legally correct. What failed was not the law itself, but the system that was supposed to ensure the jury applied it.

Here, the prosecution supplied the narrative. The judge controlled the pace of the proceedings. The defense did not interrupt, slow, or meaningfully challenge the structure of the case. No one stood up and said that the story did not add up. Silence from defense counsel functioned as concession. Jurors are trained, implicitly, to assume that if something mattered, the lawyers would highlight it. When the defense stays silent, jurors interpret that silence as confirmation.

That dynamic was reinforced by the court's rulings. Throughout the trial, defense counsel Willie Huntley repeatedly objected to the State's gun narrative and the testimony used to support it. Motions were made to strike portions of Dr McGarry's deposition. Objections were raised during voir dire, during testimony, and again during closing arguments. A motion for mistrial was filed. Each was denied or overruled. Across the entire trial record, only one objection was sustained.

From the jury's vantage point, the message was unmistakable. Challenges did not succeed. Contradictions did not interrupt the State's story. The structure of the proceedings trained jurors to assume that if something truly undermined the case, the court would stop it. Silence, enforced by rulings, functioned as validation.

That dynamic was intensified by the context of the trial itself. The jury included one Black juror. The remaining jurors were white. The State's key witness was the admitted killer who had been spared execution. Insinuation was repeated. No competing narrative was offered. Under those conditions, even attentive jurors can begin asking the wrong question, not whether the evidence proves guilt, but why the State would bring the case if it were not true.

Jurors discussed the case during breaks while testimony was still ongoing. They compared impressions of witnesses. They shared opinions about credibility and guilt before deliberations ever began. These conversations violated the most basic instructions given to every jury. None of it was reported to the court. No corrective action was taken. The discussions continued and became part of how jurors processed the case.

Their confusion surfaced in the notes they sent to the judge. The questions showed that key facts had not landed. Jurors did not understand the medical findings, even after Dr McGarry's testimony. They did not understand the chain of custody of the firearm. They did not understand Mississippi's role in the investigation or why the physical evidence did not align with the story the prosecution was telling. The record reflects not close scrutiny, but fundamental misunderstanding.

That confusion was never resolved before the verdict was taken.

When the jury returned to the courtroom, the verdict was not announced independently by the foreperson. Instead, the court recited a complete finding of guilt and asked the jury to affirm it. The structure of the exchange required confirmation, not articulation.

Each juror was required to respond individually.

At least one juror hesitated before answering. Another responded, "I guess." These were not private deliberations. They occurred in open court, on the record, at the precise moment when the law required certainty beyond a reasonable doubt.

No inquiry followed. The court did not ask for clarification. The jury was not reinstructed on the standard it had just been given. The process moved forward as if each response carried equal conviction.

In a system functioning as intended, hesitation at that moment would have mattered. Here, it carried no consequence.

Two jurors played an outsized role in shaping the verdict. One was Mari Herman. The other was the foreman she later identified, Richard McKibbon. In postconviction interviews conducted years later with volunteers working on the case, Herman explained that she and McKibbon discussed the evidence privately during the trial itself, outside the jury room and before deliberations. They evaluated testimony on their own time. They reached conclusions before the defense had finished presenting its case. These actions directly violated the court's instructions and undermined the integrity of the process.

Herman also described the climate inside the jury room once deliberations began. Jurors relied on statements that were never introduced into evidence. Others repeated rumors they had heard outside the courtroom. When no one could remember exactly what a witness had said, assumptions filled the gaps. Several jurors expressed the belief that the prosecution would not have brought the case unless it was certain. Another insisted they could not let someone dangerous walk free. The burden quietly shifted from proof beyond a reasonable doubt to imagined risk.

Bias played a role. Some jurors relied on moral judgment rather than legal standards. Others made comments about lifestyle and social relationships that had nothing to do with the evidence. A few expressed discomfort with a black man living with a white woman, views that surfaced during jury selection and should have disqualified them from service. Those attitudes shaped how

What the record shows is not simply flawed deliberation, but a jury constrained by structure. Jurors were instructed correctly but conditioned procedurally to defer. Doubt surfaced, but there was no mechanism for it to be examined. The verdict process itself required affirmation rather than judgment, leaving no space for uncertainty to interrupt the outcome.

The jury did not fail in isolation. It operated inside a system that neutralized hesitation, discouraged challenges, and treated confirmation as sufficient.

Nothing about this jury's conduct met the standard required for a fair trial. Jurors discussed the case prematurely. They relied on information outside the record. They misunderstood critical evidence. They carried bias into deliberations. And when asked to confirm their decision, at least one juror could not do so with certainty.

What emerged later was not a difference of opinion among jurors, but a process that failed at every stage where neutrality and restraint were required.

16 THE DAY THE FUTURE ENDED

On June 3, 2004, the jury filed back into the Baldwin County courtroom to deliver its verdict. Murray Jr stood as he had been instructed to do throughout the trial, facing forward, silent, waiting. His future depended on a single exchange that would take less than a minute. The courtroom was still.

Only moments earlier, the court, through Judge Wilters, had instructed the jury on the law they were required to apply. He told the jury that only strong, clear, and convincing evidence could justify a guilty verdict beyond a reasonable doubt. He instructed them that circumstantial evidence could support a conviction only if it excluded reasonable interpretations consistent with innocence and that if the evidence could equally support that someone other than the defendant committed the act, it would not be sufficient to convict.

He further instructed them that a felony conviction cannot be had on the testimony of an accomplice unless corroborated by other evidence tending to connect the defendant with the commission of the offense. Evidence that merely showed the commission of the offense or the circumstances thereof was not sufficient. Those were the governing standards placed before the jury by the court.

Before deliberations, the jury had already heard the State's closing argument.

During that argument, District Attorney John David Whetstone acknowledged the accomplice rule directly. "If all you've got in this case is the testimony of Jarius," he told the jury, "we ain't got a case. It falls like that pencil." He then proceeded as if that legal threshold had been met.

He asserted a specific time of death. "That boy's dead," he said. "He's dead at 1:20." The statement fixed time by reference to a phone call rather than medical testimony. No forensic witness was established at that time. No autopsy finding fixed it.

He addressed the abrasions on the body by invoking a general principle. "When a person dies, his heart stops beating, he doesn't bruise," he told the jury. "There could be no scrape caused by dragging him in Mississippi." He then declared location. "There could only be an abrasion where it occurred, in Foley, Alabama." The assertion treated jurisdiction as settled fact rather than a matter requiring proof.

He reinforced the State's theory by treating consistency as confirmation. He told the jury the condition of the victim's watch was "consistent with the State's theory that he was killed April 6th and dumped in Mississippi."

He then told the jury that corroboration existed throughout the case. "There's corroborative evidence all over this case that he was shot," he said, while conceding what the State did not have. "A shell casing was not found." Rather than address the absence, he instructed the jury not to require it. "That's not something that should cause you reasonable doubt," he said. "Don't try to make me prove something that I don't have to prove."

He returned again to the accomplice issue. "If all you've got in this case is the testimony of Jarius," he repeated, "we ain't got a case." He then listed what he claimed supplied the missing link. "You've got telephone, you've got speakers, and you've got threat to kill, and you've got a gun coming in." None of those items independently connected Murray Jr to the commission of the offense.

No objection interrupted the argument. No corrective instruction followed.

When the jury returned to the courtroom, the verdict form was handed up. It had been signed by the foreman, Richard McKibbon. Judge Wilters read the verdict aloud. The jury did not announce it in its own words.

The court asked, "Is this your verdict? We, the jury, find the Defendant, Murray, Jr, guilty of capital murder, intentionally killing Gary Brandon Hastings, during robbery in the first degree as charged in the indictment and as signed Richard McKibbon, foreperson?"

The structure of the question left no room for deliberation at that moment. The verdict had already been recited in full by the court. The jury was asked only to affirm what had been said to them. The jurors answered in the affirmative. The verdict was accepted.

There was no discussion of doubt on the record.

In a case built without physical evidence, without forensic proof, and without a coherent timeline tying Murray Jr to the crime, the moment carried a weight the verdict form itself could not reflect. This was not a moment of demonstrated certainty. It was a moment of finality.

What followed reflected the same pattern that had defined the trial. Throughout the proceedings, defense counsel Willie Huntley repeatedly objected to the State's gun narrative. He moved to strike portions of Dr McGarry's deposition. He objected during voir dire, during testimony, and again in closing arguments. He moved for a mistrial. Each motion was denied or overruled. Across multiple volumes of the transcript, only one objection was sustained during the entire trial.

Those rulings stood. No corrective action followed the verdict. No issue was preserved by the court's own intervention.

When the final answer was recorded, the future Murray Jr had known ended. He was twenty-two years old.

The sentence was imposed not by the jury, but by Judge Wilters. With full authority, and with access to information the defense had never been given, he sentenced Murray Jr to life without the possibility of parole. That sentence carried a finality the jury's verdict did not.

At the same time, Jarius, who had confessed to killing Brandon Hastings and whose own statements showed he acted alone, had already secured his outcome. Through a plea agreement, he avoided the death penalty and received a sentence of life with the possibility of parole. The admitted killer retained a future the law could revisit. Murray Jr did not.

The courtroom emptied after sentencing, but the moment remained fixed. Murray Sr watched from the back as deputies moved toward his son. No explanation was offered. Murray Jr was taken into custody, processed through the county facility, and placed on transport to prison.

Prison intake followed a rigid routine. Fingerprints. Photographs. An identification number. Civilian clothing replaced with the uniform worn by men sentenced to die in prison. Personal belongings were boxed and stored. Officers spoke in rehearsed commands, making clear that individuality ended at the gate.

Life without parole became the structure of Murray Jr's world beginning the moment Judge Wilters spoke it into existence and continuing through every day and year that followed. He remained where the system had placed him, held not by evidence, but by the failures that were allowed to take its place.

17 THE HARD TIME SERVED INSIDE

Immediately after the verdict, Murray Jr was placed on suicide watch at the Baldwin County Jail. He remained there for just under two months. He was isolated, monitored, and held under constant observation while the reality of life without parole set in. No explanation was given beyond procedure.

From the county jail, he was transferred to Kilby Correctional Facility to await classification. He was told the process would take sixty to ninety days.

It did not.

At Kilby, Murray Jr was placed in a one man strict lockdown cell. Meals were delivered through the door. He remained inside the cell full time except for two thirty minute breaks outside. There was no programming, no work, no movement beyond the narrow routine of confinement.

Weeks passed. Then months.

After approximately six months, Murray Jr began asking questions. Once a week, a woman visited the facility on Fridays. He asked her whether she had any information about his classification or transfer. She told him she did not. Eventually, she admitted that there was no record of movement on his case. He had not been scheduled. He had not been assigned. He had effectively been lost in the system.

She told him she would look into it.

Murray Jr remained in isolation for approximately seven months before he was finally classified and transferred.

In January 2006, he was sent to Donaldson Correctional Facility, a prison known among inmates as the West Jefferson house of pain. He remained there until June 11, 2011.

Donaldson marked the end of strict lockdown and the beginning of survival.

The environment was violent, unpredictable, and crowded with men classified among the worst offenders in the system. Murray Jr was forced to acclimate quickly. He did not seek conflict. He did not want to fight. But he learned early that avoidance alone was not always enough.

He protected himself when necessary and worked to maintain a reputation as someone who did not cause trouble. That reputation mattered inside. It reduced attention. It reduced targeting. It did not eliminate risk.

He still received a small number of disciplinary citations. One involved an accusation of contraband found in his bed. The substance was salt. It belonged to another inmate. The bed had been misidentified. The citation stood anyway.

Another involved an accusation of failure to obey a direct order. A guard gave Murray Jr permission to go to the barber. When he arrived, a lieutenant questioned why he was there. He explained that he had been given permission. The guard denied it in front of the lieutenant. Murray Jr was written up. The citation functioned to protect the guard, not to correct misconduct.

During his time at Donaldson, Murray Jr earned his GED. He worked in the infirmary and later in hospice, caring for inmates nearing the end of their lives. He held other jobs as available.

It was also during these years that exhaustion set in. Murray Jr tried to understand his postconviction options. He tried to make sense of how to prove his innocence within a system that offered no guidance and no timeline. Hope became harder to sustain. The effort to fight legally while surviving daily confinement wore him down.

In 2011, Murray Jr was transferred to Holman Correctional Facility.

The transfer required starting over again.

He was initially placed in general population with some of the most dangerous inmates in the system. For months, he lived in an environment that required constant vigilance. Violence was a daily possibility. Murray Jr learned to watch his surroundings, protect himself, and avoid escalation whenever possible.

Holman Correctional Facility was later documented publicly for its conditions. Rows of bunks packed tightly together. Concrete walls that amplified sound. A dorm that never truly rested.

The building trapped heat during the summer months and allowed cold air to move freely through the structure in winter. Ventilation was poor. Noise was constant. Privacy did not exist. Mail was inspected. Phone calls were limited and monitored. Visits required long drives, long waits, and conversations under continuous observation.

Every hour was governed by counts, schedules, and restrictions that reinforced the absence of autonomy.

Despite the environment, Murray Jr maintained an exceptional disciplinary record. He received only one violation during his time at Holman, and that was for fighting in self defense without a weapon.

His classification level reflected that record. Although life without parole inmates are typically assigned the highest security classification, Murray's security level was reduced to Level 1. This designation is rare for prisoners serving life without parole.

His behavior allowed him to move into the Honor Dorm.

The Honor Dorm housed men with stable conduct and lower risk profiles. Compared to general population, it was calmer. Murray Jr worked a variety of jobs over the years, including kitchen duty, laundry, and beginning in 2020, work in the sewing plant.

During these years, Murray Jr consistently sought out every form of education and self improvement available to him. He completed academic coursework, vocational training, financial literacy programs, meditation and mental discipline courses, medical education classes, and faith based study. He earned recognition for leadership and conduct, including being named Resident of the Month and Crewmember of the Month for education programs. These were not isolated efforts. They reflected a sustained pattern over many years of using the only tools available to him to remain grounded, disciplined, and engaged with life inside prison. A verified list of completed programs appears later in this book.

This matters because it shows who Murray Jr was when the system still allowed growth. Before overcrowding erased structure and before life without parole hardened into pure stagnation, Murray did exactly what the system claims it wants incarcerated people to do. He participated. He learned. He contributed.

Around 2020, conditions changed again.

At approximately the same time the Department of Justice conducted an audit of Holman, four general population dorms were condemned. The dorms, identified as A, B, C, and D, each housed approximately one hundred fourteen inmates, all serving life sentences, some with parole eligibility and some without.

Those dorms remain condemned as of January 2026.

The inmates from those four dorms were either transferred to other facilities or crammed into existing housing. Many were placed into the Honor Dorm. Additional bunk beds were added until the population reached approximately one hundred ninety two men in a space never designed to hold that number.

Murray Jr described the dorm as a chicken coop, commonly referred to as the barn.

Overcrowding intensified. Privacy disappeared entirely. Behavioral classifications were mixed. Noise increased. Tension increased.

Around the same period, programming was eliminated.

For inmates serving life without parole, confinement became static. No classes. No structured activity. No pathway to progress.

In July 2025, Murray Jr lost his job at the sewing plant. He was told it was due to budget constraints and lack of materials. He had started earning thirty cents an hour. By the time he was laid off, he earned approximately one dollar and fifteen cents an hour.

Without income, Murray Jr became dependent on outside support to afford basic commissary items. Volunteers began sending funds so he could purchase necessities.

As of this writing, Murray Jr remains housed in an overcrowded dorm with mixed behavior levels, no job, no programming, and no privacy.

This is the environment in which he serves life without parole.

The punishment is not only the length of the sentence. It is the daily conditions under which it is lived.

18 THE LONG FAILURE OF POSTCONVICTION

The years after Murray Jr's conviction did not bring review, reconsideration, or any meaningful attempt to correct the failures that had shaped his case. They marked a long decline in which every safeguard meant to protect the innocent eroded through delay, disengagement, and silence.

Murray Jr was twenty-one when he was arrested on 04/23/2003. By the time his conviction was entered in 2005, he had already lost two years of freedom. From that point forward, the postconviction process stretched across nearly two decades with almost no substantive legal action taken on his behalf.

The direct appeal should have forced a court to confront the contradictions embedded in the trial record. Witness statements that shifted under pressure. The distortion of the Mississippi autopsy. The introduction of an unrelated gun. The absence of any Alabama medical examination. None of those issues were meaningfully addressed. The appeal moved forward mechanically, offering the appearance of review without its substance.

The next avenue for relief was a Rule 32 petition, Alabama's postconviction process and the only state level opportunity to raise suppressed evidence and constitutional violations after a direct appeal has ended. Once a Rule 32 petition is denied, the state courts are closed, and no further review is available within Alabama.

It was filed by Wilmer E Huntley, the same attorney who had conducted no investigation at trial, called no alibi witnesses, challenged no forensic claims, and allowed Murray Jr to sit through testimony he could not hear. Huntley was not court appointed. He was privately retained by the Lawrence family who mortgaged their home and continued to receive payment long after trial, even as no meaningful postconviction work was performed.

Filing the petition was the only step he took. He sought no discovery. He requested no hearing. He gathered no affidavits. He raised no claims that required scrutiny of his own performance. The petition sat untouched until it effectively died from neglect. No judge ever examined a single allegation inside it.

After Huntley, three additional attorneys were hired between the mid-2000s and late 2010s. Each entered the case promising action. Not one reconstructed a timeline. Not one undertook a serious examination of the Mississippi autopsy. Not one challenged the firearm narrative that had replaced it. Time passed while the case stood still.

As these failures accumulated, Murray Jr's capacity for hope eroded. Letters that once carried optimism shifted into resignation. Attorneys appeared and disappeared without action. Years passed with no hearing, no progress, no review. Whatever expectation he once held that the courts would eventually correct what had gone wrong faded into something quieter and heavier.

By late 2022, nineteen and a half years after he first lost his freedom, postconviction relief had not simply stalled. It had evaporated. This collapse was not the result of a single ruling or denial. It was the product of a sustained pattern of inaction that left Murray Jr exactly where he had been since 04/23/2003.

19 THE DISCOVERY OF SUPPRESSED EVIDENCE IN 2023

For twenty years, the case was understood to rest on a narrow and uncontested record. Mississippi recovered Brandon Hastings's body in Vancleave, Mississippi, near the Jackson County line. Mississippi documented the scene and performed the only autopsy. That understanding did not unravel until May 23, 2023.

In the course of reexamining physical distances and retracing movements from 2003, volunteers traveled to Jackson County, Mississippi, to time the specific route Jarius described. The drive was measured from the alleged shooting location off County Road 49 in Foley, Alabama, to Murray Jr's residence, and then from that residence to the remote site near Vancleave where Brandon Hastings's body was found. The purpose was precise. Measure the actual distance. Confirm the terrain. Determine whether the movements described at trial were physically plausible within the documented timeline.

The work was methodical. It required maps, recorded testimony, and on the ground verification. It required asking questions in person and following details wherever they led. It was the kind of foundational investigative effort that ordinarily occurs at the beginning of a homicide case.

While in Jackson County, volunteers made additional inquiries about the area where Brandon's body had been recovered. The location was near Vancleave, not far from the Mississippi state line. At the Vancleave Police Department and the Gautier Police Department, no one initially recognized the Jarius name. At the local post offices, no confirmation was immediately available. It was only when an older man pulled into the Gautier post office parking lot and was asked directly that a different answer emerged. He confirmed that members of the McNeil family had long lived in that corridor, extending toward the state line.

That geographic detail reframed the dump site. The location was not random. It was familiar ground.

While reviewing timelines and rechecking narrow details already believed to be settled, a volunteer contacted a member of the Hastings family to clarify a minor point. The call was not confrontational. It was intended to confirm a detail already believed to be understood.

The family member hesitated. He made clear that he did not want to revisit the entire story. He did not want the case reopened in conversation. He expressed concern that revisiting details would stir up issues the family had tried to put to rest.

During that hesitation, he suggested there were aspects of Brandon's personal life that had been misunderstood or misrepresented over the years. His comments implied that Brandon's relationships had been more complicated than publicly acknowledged. He did not state this directly. He did not elaborate. He did not want to.

The volunteer did not press that subject. The original question was repeated, carefully.

That was when the response changed.

"They dug Brandon's body up."

The statement came without hesitation, delivered as though it were common knowledge. It was not. No attorney who had worked on the case over two decades knew of it. No transcript referenced it. No filing disclosed it. No discovery response hinted at it. Murray Jr. had never been told. Neither had his family. No advocate had encountered it anywhere in the record.

The volunteer asked again, carefully, to be certain of what was meant.

"You mean the body was exhumed?"

The family member confirmed it. Brandon Hastings's body had been taken out of the ground after burial. The order authorizing disinterment was signed by Judge Robert Wilters during the period when the prosecution was preparing its case. According to the family member, those present included personnel from the Baldwin County Sheriff's Office and staff from Mack Funeral Home, which handled the physical removal and reinterment of the body. No Mississippi authority was present. No Mississippi coroner. No Mississippi forensic pathologist. The family was never told why the exhumation was done.

What he described did not resemble a legitimate forensic procedure.

The body was exhumed, opened, examined, and reburied.

No report was generated. No findings were documented. Nothing was logged. Nothing was disclosed to the defense.

When asked what paperwork the family had received, the answer was simple.

"We never saw any. They just told us it had been done."

That response fractured the foundation of the case.

If an exhumation occurred, Alabama accessed Brandon Hastings's remains after burial without producing records, without documenting purpose or findings, and without notifying the defense. If information from that examination was used to shape the prosecution's theory while remaining undisclosed, its suppression altered the evidentiary landscape before trial ever began.

Within days, public records requests were filed across Baldwin County agencies. The responses were evasive and contradictory. Some offices claimed no records existed. Others said they did not know who would have them. No agency acknowledged responsibility. No one produced documentation.

Only after the issue was escalated with reference to possible legal action did Baldwin County issue a carefully worded admission that an exhumation had occurred. The disclosure followed a public records request that had not asked for an autopsy. A volunteer requested a coroner's report, believing it might reflect another examination. Had an autopsy been requested, the likely response would have been that none existed. Instead, the narrower request produced the admission that the body had been exhumed.

Even then, no date was provided. No photographs. No report. No chain of custody. No explanation of what was done or what was found.

Which meant one thing. The exhumation itself was suppressed evidence.

Its existence was withheld.

Its purpose was withheld.

Its results were withheld.

This was not an administrative oversight. It was an omission that protected the prosecution's narrative.

With that knowledge, moments from the trial that had long felt disjointed came into focus. The insinuations about a gunshot injury. The questions that suggested knowledge beyond the Mississippi autopsy. The vague references to reviewing injuries without stating how or when. What once sounded like speculation now aligned with information drawn from an undisclosed examination.

Mississippi documented no firearm injury. Mississippi retained custody. Mississippi performed the only lawful autopsy.

Yet Brandon Hastings's body had been reopened without disclosure, and whatever was learned was never shared.

When that truth surfaced in May 2023, the nature of the fight changed. The effort was no longer confined to exposing a flawed investigation. It now confronted a system that had taken physical control of the victim's body, concealed the act, and allowed the case to proceed as though nothing had occurred.

The truth had been buried twice.

Once in the ground.

Once in the record.

20 THE IMPLICATIONS OF SUPPRESSED EVIDENCE

The discovery of the exhumation did not add a new theory to the case. It exposed what had already been done.

For years, the prosecution's case had relied on suggestion rather than proof. The Mississippi autopsy was treated as incomplete. The cause of death was framed as uncertain. Questions were asked that implied knowledge beyond what had been documented. Jurors were left to assume that Alabama possessed information Mississippi did not.

The undisclosed exhumation explained how those implications entered the courtroom.

If Brandon Hastings's body was opened and examined after burial, and if the results of that examination were never disclosed to the defense, then the trial did not proceed on a complete record. It proceeded on a curated one. Information known to the State but withheld from the defense shaped the narrative without ever being tested.

That is the essence of suppression.

Evidence does not have to be favorable on its face to be material. Its value lies in its existence. The defense has the right to know what was done, what was found, and what conclusions were drawn, especially when the State uses implication to fill gaps it cannot prove.

Here, the implications were everywhere.

The prosecution referenced injuries without identifying their source. It suggested uncertainty where Mississippi had documented none. It leaned into a firearm narrative despite the absence of any gunshot wound. These were not neutral ambiguities. They were directional cues.

Without disclosure, the defense could not challenge the legitimacy of any Alabama examination. It could not question who authorized it. It could not explore whether it contradicted or confirmed Mississippi's findings. It could not expose the absence of documentation. It could not show the jury that an act had occurred without process, record, or accountability.

The jury never learned that Alabama had gone back into the body.

The jury never learned that nothing was documented.

The jury never learned that whatever was done was kept from the defense.

Instead, jurors were left with the impression that the State's case rested on a fuller forensic picture than the one presented. That impression was false.

Suppression is not measured by whether the State believes the evidence mattered. It is measured by whether the defense was denied the opportunity to confront it. Here, the denial was total.

The consequences extend beyond one omission.

An undisclosed exhumation undermines the integrity of every forensic inference made at trial. It contaminates the narrative built around cause of death. It raises questions about what information influenced charging decisions, witness preparation, and courtroom strategy. It casts doubt on the legitimacy of proceedings that depended on silence where disclosure was required.

By withholding the act itself, the State insulated its narrative from scrutiny.

What appeared, for years, as a case built on weak evidence, now revealed itself as something more troubling. A case in which evidence was not merely overlooked but removed from view. A case in which physical access to the victim's body occurred outside the record, outside the defense's knowledge, and outside the adversarial process entirely.

Once that reality was understood, the frame of the case shifted.

This was no longer a question of whether mistakes had been made. It was a question of how a prosecution proceeded while concealing an act that should have altered everything that followed.

The suppressed evidence did not sit at the margins of the case.

It sat at its center.

21 THE EVIDENCE THAT "DID NOT MATTER"

The exhumation and subsequent Alabama forensic examination did not occur in isolation. Responsibility for authorizing, carrying out, and concealing that examination flowed through the same network of officials who controlled the investigation and prosecution. Judge Robert Wilters signed the order authorizing the disinterment. Huey Mack Sr, then Baldwin County Coroner and owner of Mack Funeral Home, authorized the examination under authority cited from the District Attorney's Office. Mack Funeral Home carried out the physical handling of the remains. Huey Mack Jr, then a senior officer within the Baldwin County Sheriff's Office and later sheriff, was a central investigative figure in the case. No record reflects that any of these individuals required disclosure of the examination or its results to the defense.

Their explanations varied in phrasing but converged in theme.

When contacted after the records surfaced, former Baldwin County District Attorney John David Whetstone, who personally prosecuted Murray Jr, acknowledged that Alabama had examined the body. He then dismissed its significance.

"It wouldn't have mattered," Whetstone said. "It didn't uncover anything new."

That statement is now part of the public record.

In the same conversation, Whetstone acknowledged that the Alabama examination did not contradict the Mississippi autopsy. He confirmed that it was consistent with Mississippi's findings.

That admission carries unavoidable weight.

Mississippi's autopsies concluded that Brandon Hastings died from asphyxiation due to ligature strangulation and found no evidence of a gunshot wound. An Alabama forensic examination that reinforced those findings necessarily failed to support the gunshot narrative advanced at trial.

Yet the jury was never told that Alabama had already examined the body and found no gunshot injury. Instead, the prosecution used the implication of Alabama involvement to suggest forensic uncertainty.

When presented with the signed motion to disinter remains bearing his name and the correspondence transmitting the Alabama findings to his office, Whetstone stated that he did not recall ordering the examination and did not remember receiving the report.

"I don't like second opinions," he said.

He suggested that the request may have been initiated by an assistant district attorney or carried out under authority delegated to Huey Mack Sr, then Baldwin County Coroner and owner of Mack Funeral Home. Despite these explanations, Whetstone acknowledged that if such an examination occurred and produced findings, the defense should have received them.

He also acknowledged that he should have received them himself.

The position did not change.

"It wouldn't have mattered."

The same framing was later offered by the sitting Baldwin County District Attorney, who stated that the Alabama examination "did not uncover anything new" and therefore would not have changed the outcome of the case.

No official disputed that the examination occurred.
No official disputed that it was authorized.

No official disputed that it failed to identify a gunshot wound. No official disputed that it aligned with Mississippi's autopsy.

Instead, the explanation offered was that its existence was insignificant.

That explanation does not resolve the suppression. It confirms it.

Evidence does not become optional because the prosecution believes it is unhelpful. The State does not get to decide, after the fact, that evidence favorable to the defense is immaterial. That determination belongs to the defense and, ultimately, to the court.

Responsibility did not rest with one person alone.

Judge Robert Wilters signed the order authorizing the disinterment. By doing so, he had actual knowledge that an exhumation and forensic examination were taking place. There is no record that he required confirmation that the results were disclosed to the defense. There is no record that the jury was informed of the examination's existence. When suppression issues later arose, Wilters denied relief without addressing the undisclosed Alabama forensic examination.

Huey Mack Sr authorized the examination under authority cited from the District Attorney's Office. Huey Mack Jr, then a senior officer in the Baldwin County Sheriff's Office and later sheriff, was a central investigative figure in the case. The record reflects no objection from either to the nondisclosure of the examination or its results.

Every institutional safeguard that should have prevented this outcome was present.

Every one of them failed.

Defense attorney Willie Huntley later stated that he never received the Alabama examination report and did not know that Brandon

Hastings's body had been exhumed. He stated that had he known, he would have acted differently.

Years later, when the records surfaced, none of the officials involved claimed that the Alabama examination supported a gunshot theory. One acknowledged that it reinforced Mississippi's findings. Yet the implication of Alabama involvement, stripped of its contents, had been used at trial to suggest the opposite.

The contradiction remains unresolved.

The explanation offered was not that the examination did not exist. It was that it did not matter.

And yet the State's own examination confirmed that Brandon Hastings was not killed by a gun.

That fact was withheld from the defense.
That fact was withheld from the jury.
That fact is why this evidence mattered.

Read Lagniappe's "Dig Deep" article by Rob Holbert from October 4, 2023

At the time the Lagniappe article was published, it was reasonable to assume that the exhumation of Brandon Hastings's body meant a second autopsy had been performed. In ordinary homicide investigations, disinterment is undertaken for the purpose of conducting a full forensic autopsy or reexamination, and the trial record itself repeatedly insinuated that Alabama had conducted its own forensic review.

Subsequent records obtained through public records requests clarified that this assumption was incorrect. There was only one lawful autopsy, performed by Mississippi authorities. The Alabama examination conducted after exhumation did not constitute a second autopsy, did not establish a new cause of death, and did not contradict Mississippi's findings in any respect. It produced no evidence of a gunshot wound and no forensic support for the firearm narrative presented at trial.

The significance of the exhumation is not that it produced a different forensic conclusion. It is that the examination occurred at all, was authorized by court order, failed to support the prosecution's theory, and was never disclosed to the defense or the jury. The State nonetheless referenced Alabama's involvement at trial in a manner that suggested independent or conflicting forensic findings, an implication the records do not support.

22 TAKING THE EVIDENCE TO THE STATE

Maxwell Tillman Law Group LLC, based in Birmingham, Alabama, was retained by advocates working in concert with the Lawrence family after suppressed evidence had been identified, organized, and delivered in usable form. The decision to hire the firm was deliberate and informed. It followed years of inaction by prior counsel and came only after advocates had reconstructed timelines, assembled transcripts, gathered forensic records, and produced a written analysis summarizing suppressed evidence and the contradictions it exposed.

Before agreeing to take the case, Maxwell Tillman spoke directly with Murray Sr. He stated clearly that he would not take a case he could not win. The representation was unqualified. It was made with full knowledge that the conviction was final, that the sentence was life without parole, and that success would require confronting the State with evidence that had never been disclosed to the jury.

Once retained, Tillman assigned the Rule 32 litigation to Gabrielle Humber, an associate at the firm. While there was ongoing communication with Humber, it was Tillman himself who had been hired and who had made the initial representations to the family.

By the time counsel entered the case, advocates had already spent thousands of hours reviewing transcripts, reconstructing timelines, analyzing forensic records, and documenting suppressed evidence. This work was turned over to the firm in organized form so litigation could proceed without delay and be presented through an evidentiary hearing, the stage at which evidence and witnesses are formally examined by the court. Counsel was not being asked to discover facts. Counsel was being asked to litigate facts already uncovered.

The Rule 32 petition moved forward without the development the process is designed to require. No discovery requests were filed. No motion to compel was submitted. No affidavits were secured from witnesses whose statements had shifted or whose accounts had never been formally locked into the record. Despite the availability of witnesses, documents, and a detailed roadmap provided by advocates, the factual foundation necessary to force an evidentiary hearing was not built.

During this period, Humber traveled to the Baldwin County District Attorney's Office as part of the firm's handling of the Rule 32 litigation. The visit provided direct access to the prosecuting authority and its files. Even with that access, no discovery was obtained. No materials were produced. No forensic records were released. No internal communications were disclosed. No follow up motion was filed to compel production. The State retained exclusive control over its files, and the Rule 32 record reflects no effort to challenge that imbalance.

The State filed its response to the Rule 32 petition under the name of Kristi Hagood, an Assistant District Attorney employed under District Attorney Robert Wilters. At the time, Hagood was assigned to the Child Advocacy Unit, a division that prosecutes child abuse, elder abuse, and financial exploitation cases, not homicide cases and not postconviction litigation. Despite the gravity of the claims and her lack of experience in wrongful conviction litigation, she was selected to respond to a petition alleging forensic suppression, witness coercion, and constitutional failure.

The State's response denied relief without engaging the substance of what had been raised. It did not address the Mississippi autopsy, which concluded death by ligature strangulation. It did not explain the absence of any Alabama autopsy. It did not confront documented witness coercion or testimony altered under pressure. It did not address the indictment's lack of a valid signature. Instead, it rejected the claims in general terms and moved forward without grappling with the evidentiary contradictions that had finally been assembled.

The response also misstated critical timeline facts central to the petition. It asserted, without citation, that Murray Jr picked up Jarius on the night Brandon Hastings was killed. The record showed otherwise. Call records, witness statements, and reconstructed timelines established that any contact between Murray Jr and Jarius occurred the following night, not the night of the homicide. This distinction was not minor. It removed Murray Jr from proximity, opportunity, and participation in the crime itself. The State's response did not reconcile this contradiction or acknowledge the underlying record.

The response further implied joint activity between Murray Jr and Jarius during the critical window of the homicide without citing any evidence placing Murray Jr with Brandon Hastings, at the scene, or in possession of the victim's property. It treated implication as fact and ignored the absence of forensic, eyewitness, or physical evidence tying Murray Jr to the crime. These misstatements directly affected the theory of guilt by proximity that had already failed at trial.

After the State filed its response, volunteer advocates prepared detailed counter arguments addressing the State's factual omissions and mischaracterizations. These counter arguments were specific. They walked through the autopsy record, the timeline errors, the witness statement shifts, the absence of forensic support, and the procedural defects the State had avoided. They were delivered to counsel with the clear expectation that they would be filed as a rebuttal and joined to the Rule 32 record.

Advocates followed up to confirm that the rebuttal would be filed. No confirmation was received. No explanation was provided for the omission. No alternative strategy was communicated. No rebuttal memorandum appears in the docket. No response answering the State's filing was submitted. The counter arguments prepared by advocates were left entirely outside the court record.

In postconviction litigation, that silence carries consequences. When the State files a response and the defense does not answer, courts treat the unanswered assertions as unpressed and resolved. The record closes with the State's version left uncontested, regardless of whether contrary evidence exists.

Judge Robert Wilters accepted the State's response without a hearing, without inquiry, and without requiring the unanswered contradictions to be joined to the record. He was not an appellate judge encountering the case for the first time. He presided over Murray Jr's trial. He imposed a life without parole sentence. He later accepted the State's postconviction response without ordering discovery, without compelling rebuttal, and without subjecting the claims to adversarial testing.

None of these omissions resulted from a lack of evidence. The information existed. It was known to investigators and prosecutors. It was available to counsel. It was provided in organized form. It was followed up on. It was simply not joined to the record.

What the court reviewed was incomplete; what the record preserved was one sided; what remained untested was the truth.

The record now establishes that a case containing this volume of contradiction was allowed to close without scrutiny. And once that question is asked, another follows naturally. If this record could pass through the system without correction, how many others have done the same?

23 THE REBUTTAL COUNSEL FAILED TO FILE

The State's response, which is the prosecution's written opposition to a postconviction petition, did not simply oppose relief. It reconstructed the record in ways that blurred timelines, shifted emphasis away from exculpatory testimony, and relied on implication where the trial record showed absence. If that response was left unrebutted, the court would hear only the State's version of events.

Volunteer advocates prepared counter arguments to prevent that outcome.

Those counter arguments were not narrative commentary. They were citation-based rebuttals grounded in the trial transcript, exhibits, phone records, forensic findings, and sworn testimony. They were written to answer the State's factual assertions point by point and to correct errors that, if uncontested, would be treated as settled fact.

The counter arguments first addressed errors in the State's "Statement of the Facts." The State's response blurred who last saw Brandon Hastings alive by shifting focus toward his mother's last sighting at approximately 8:00 pm on 04/05/2003. The counter arguments corrected this by citing testimony that Debra Fudge saw Brandon alive at approximately 1:30 am on 04/06/2003 at Bebo's Car Wash in Foley, seated in his Acura with Jarius. They further noted that Fudge identified Jarius in a police lineup but was never called as a witness at Murray Jr's trial.

The counter arguments corrected the State's framing that Jarius merely "helped" plan the robbery. They documented that Jarius pled as the sole actor at his 05/14/2003 bench trial, admitting responsibility for the robbery and homicide, and later altered his account only after renewed exposure to capital punishment. They cited phone records showing no evidence that Murray Jr coordinated a lure, received Brandon's phone number, or communicated with Brandon at all.

They highlighted internal contradictions in Jarius's gun narrative, including shifting descriptions of where Brandon was allegedly shot. These inconsistencies were tied directly to the absence of any firearm injury in the Mississippi autopsy, which the State's response minimized rather than confronted.

The counter arguments corrected the timeline of contact between Jarius and Murray Jr. They documented that the record showed no contact between them during the critical window of the homicide and that Jarius's cell service was disconnected, requiring payphones or third-party phones. They tied this to the documented call Jarius made to Brandon from Elizabeth Mixson's landline.

They further documented that Cynthia Weston testified she called Jarius a day or two later after his cell service had been restored and that she did not provide money for that restoration, consistent with robbery proceeds being used.

The counter arguments addressed the firearm narrative separately from the cause of death. They traced the gun's origin and movement through Jarius's hands and documented how testimony later reframed that gun as a murder weapon despite no forensic support. They identified this shift as narrative retrofitting rather than evidence.

They addressed selective witness reliance by the State, noting the resurrection of Kathleen Blair Gordon while minimizing or omitting testimony from witnesses whose accounts placed Murray Jr elsewhere or contradicted the State's theory. They also addressed the State's emphasis on drug use as prejudicial and unsupported.

They corrected narrative framing related to video surveillance, payphone proximity, and Elizabeth Mixson's testimony, including a typographical error in the State's response listing an incorrect date.

On forensics, the counter arguments rejected the gunshot theory as conjecture and compiled what was missing, no bullet, no shell casing, no gunpowder residue, no blood trail, no DNA, no fingerprints, and no established crime scene. They tied this directly to trial testimony maintaining death by ligature strangulation.

The most consequential error addressed by the counter arguments was the State's misstatement of date.

The State's response asserted that Murray Lawrence Jr picked up Jarius on the night Brandon Hastings was killed. This was false. The counter arguments documented that the pickup occurred the following night, after Jarius called and asked to be picked up. Murray Jr went with him to Brooks Miller's house because he was scared and did not know what to do. He did not know why Jarius wanted to meet and believed Jarius was up to something.

This error was not incidental. By shifting the pickup to the night of the homicide, the State placed Murray Jr into the critical window of time, manufacturing proximity, opportunity, and implied participation where none existed. Correcting the date removed Murray Jr entirely from the crime itself. The contact occurred after the homicide and did not place him at the scene, in planning, or in execution.

That error was not minor. It removed Murray Jr from proximity, opportunity, and participation in the crime itself. Left unanswered, it allowed the State to imply involvement where the record excluded it.

All of these counter arguments were compiled, organized, cited, and delivered to counsel. Counsel did not need to investigate, reconstruct the record, or develop new theories. Counsel needed only to respond to the State's Rule 32 filing by placing the rebuttal into the record.

Advocates followed up repeatedly asking whether the counter arguments had been filed. They were given no indication that they had not. They were left to assume the response had been made.

None of the counter arguments were filed. None were attached to the Rule 32 record. None were addressed by the court.

As a result, the State's misstatements, omissions, and framing choices went unanswered. The court ruled on an incomplete record in which the most direct factual corrections were never joined, never tested, and never considered.

The failure was not the absence of evidence. The failure was the absence of response.

24 THE RECORD CLOSED WITHOUT OPPOSITION

Moving to the Alabama Supreme Court did not occur in a vacuum. It happened because the Rule 32 process had failed at every point where it was supposed to engage the evidence. The State's response avoided the substance. No rebuttal was required. The circuit court ruled without demanding answers. The Court of Criminal Appeals affirmed without resolving the factual disputes raised. Escalation was not strategic. It was unavoidable.

By the time the case reached the Alabama Supreme Court, there was no illusion left about what was at stake. State remedies were nearly exhausted. Federal deadlines loomed. This was the last door inside Alabama's court system, and everyone involved understood that what happened here would shape everything that followed. The Supreme Court stage existed for one reason only, to force unresolved factual disputes into the record before procedural closure made silence permanent.

A Petition for Writ of Certiorari was filed, a formal request asking the Alabama Supreme Court to review the decision of the Court of Criminal Appeals and determine whether it had committed a legal error requiring correction.

On its face, it appeared substantial. Dozens of pages. Constitutional claims. Citations. References to suppressed evidence, coerced testimony, and failures that had defined the case for more than two decades. Life without parole hung in the balance.

But when the petition was later examined carefully, after the firm stepped away and the advocates were forced to take over the work themselves, something critical became clear. It was not immediately apparent at the time.

Nothing new had been added.

The arguments presented to the Alabama Supreme Court were not developed for discretionary review. They were not reframed to challenge the reasoning of the Court of Criminal Appeals. They did not identify a specific legal error requiring correction. They did not explain why the case presented an issue of broader constitutional importance beyond the denial of Rule 32 relief.

Instead, the filing repeated the Rule 32 petition almost verbatim.

The structure was the same.
The sequencing was the same.
The language was the same.
Only the caption at the top of the page had changed.

This distinction is not technical. It is foundational. A cert petition is not a second Rule 32 filing. It serves a different purpose, addresses a different court, and operates under different standards. The function of certiorari is not to reargue the trial record, but to explain why the lower appellate court got it wrong in a way that demands intervention. Any firm practicing postconviction law knows this or should.

The Alabama Supreme Court almost never grants cert unless three core requirements are met. First, the petition must identify a legal error in the decision of the Court of Criminal Appeals. Second, it must explain why that error matters beyond the individual case and warrants discretionary review. Third, it must present something new for the Court to engage with, a legal question or conflict that has not already been resolved.

This petition met none of those requirements because it was, in substance, a refiled Rule 32.

From the Court's perspective, the posture was simple. The Court of Criminal Appeals had already affirmed the denial of relief. The petitioner was now asking the Supreme Court to reread the same arguments without being told why intervention was required. That posture invites a summary denial.

The response came back as a single page.

No opinion.
No analysis.
No engagement with the claims.

A discretionary refusal to review.

This was not a ruling on the merits. It was not an evaluation of the constitutional claims. It was a decision not to engage at all, consistent with how the Alabama Supreme Court handles cert petitions that fail to present a new legal question or a compelling reason to intervene.

What makes this moment consequential is not simply that review was denied. It is why it was denied.

The constitutional claims were never meaningfully addressed. Newly raised evidence was never analyzed. Unresolved factual disputes were never confronted by the state's highest court. The door closed not because the issues lacked weight, but because the advocacy did not require the Court to open it.

This is the point where competent representation matters most. And it is the point where it failed again.

Submitting a substantively unchanged filing at this stage all but guarantees a summary denial. That is not hindsight. It is baseline appellate practice. The decision to proceed this way stripped the case of its final opportunity for substantive state level engagement.

When the Alabama Supreme Court issued its certificate of judgment on 6 13 2025, state remedies were technically exhausted. But nothing had been substantively reviewed. Murray Lawrence Jr was now trapped in the narrow space between state closure and unforgiving federal deadlines, with no reasoning to challenge and no findings to rebut.

At that moment, Murray Jr remained incarcerated, with no access to court dockets, no ability to track filings, and no independent way to know whether the final door inside Alabama's court system had closed. He depended entirely on the lawyers retained to protect his case.

Notice of the denial did not arrive immediately. Murray Jr and the advocates working on his behalf learned of the ruling only after repeated follow-up inquiries, not through any direct communication explaining what had occurred or why state review had ended.

Continuity mattered more than anything else at that moment. Federal deadlines do not pause for confusion, burnout, or law firm dysfunction. The ninety-day clock to preserve federal review had begun.

Approximately one week after the State's response, and only after repeated follow up by advocates, Maxwell disclosed that the firm had received the filing more than a week earlier. No response had been made. No plan had been shared. No explanation had been offered while days passed and deadlines advanced.

During that same period, Gabrielle Humber ceased working on Murray Jr's case. No notice of withdrawal was provided to Murray Jr. No transition occurred. No supplemental filing was made. No pending deadlines were disclosed.

The Alabama Supreme Court's denial issued without any additional advocacy on Murray Jr's behalf.

At the same time, other incarcerated clients represented by Humber at Holman Prison reported that their matters had similarly gone dormant. Murray Jr learned of her departure not through formal notice, but through word of mouth inside the prison.

Months later, Humber publicly promoted professional success and positive client feedback unrelated to Murray Jr's case. She remains in active practice and relocated to Panama City, Florida.

Maxwell stated that he would personally handle the next stage of the case. Time passed. Days turned into weeks. No filings appeared. No guidance was given.

Then a letter arrived.

In that letter, Maxwell advised the family that his firm might not be the right fit and that they should seek new counsel. The letter contained no case transfer, no list of pending deadlines, and no assistance locating substitute representation. It arrived after significant time had already elapsed.

By the time the letter was received, roughly sixty days remained of the original ninety-day federal window. That window was not workable for a life without parole case involving decades of procedural history, thousands of pages of records, and unresolved filings. No attorney could realistically step in, absorb the record, and act without jeopardizing the case.

The abandonment carried legal consequences. Alabama's Rules of Professional Conduct require an attorney to keep a client reasonably informed, to protect the client's interests upon termination, and to take reasonable steps to avoid foreseeable prejudice. That includes timely notice, transfer of the case file, disclosure of deadlines, and cooperation in securing substitute counsel. None of those obligations were met.

Murray was left without representation at the precise moment federal deadlines became unforgiving. A bar complaint would later be filed. But complaints do not stop clocks.

25 WHY WAS JUSTICE NOT POSSIBLE IN ALABAMA?

Many of the individuals whose actions shaped this case remain in office. Some hold higher positions than they did then. Others occupy roles that benefit from the continued suppression of how this case was handled. Accountability here would not fall on one mistake or one actor. It would expose a network of decisions, omissions, and protections that made correction inconvenient and silence safer.

The same institutions and individuals appeared repeatedly across critical stages of the case. The sheriff's office, the coroner, investigators, prosecutors, and the funeral home operated within a closed loop of authority, with no meaningful separation between custodial control, investigative decision making, and narrative formation. This overlap did not require coordination or conspiracy. It functioned through continuity of roles and shared institutional interest, ensuring that no independent checkpoint ever disrupted the trajectory of the case.

The wrongful conviction of Murray Jr did not come from a single decision or a single official. It came from a network of power inside Baldwin County that protected its own, rewarded loyalty, and advanced the very people who shaped the case. The result is a system where the individuals tied to the original investigation and prosecution not only kept their positions but rose into roles with broader influence.

Understanding what happened to Murray Jr requires understanding who benefited from the system that failed him, and where they are today.

Justice also depends on adversarial enforcement. Courts do not test evidence on their own initiative. Prosecutors are not required to challenge themselves. When defense counsel fails to investigate, fails to confront contradictions, or fails to preserve the record, the system does not correct the imbalance. It absorbs it. In Murray Jr's case, the absence of meaningful defense advocacy at critical stages did not counterbalance institutional power. It enabled it. That failure was not separate from the system described here. It was one of the conditions that allowed it to operate without resistance.

At the time of the investigation, information later obtained through interviews reflected that Jarius was not open about his sexual orientation with friends or family. Those same interviews confirmed that his father was a retired United States Marshal. The record contains no direct evidence that his father intervened, requested protection, or influenced investigative or prosecutorial decisions. What the record does show is a case in which questions that would normally be asked were not asked, scrutiny that would normally follow did not occur, and a witness whose credibility determined the outcome was treated as untouchable. The relevance is not causation, but context. It helps explain why pressure moved in one direction only, and why reversal of course never triggered examination.

The clearest example is Robert Wilters, the judge who presided over Murray Jr's trial. He watched the prosecution present a gunshot theory that contradicted the Mississippi autopsy. He permitted coerced statements, unsigned indictments, shifting testimony, and evidence introduced without foundation. He allowed a narrative to take root in his courtroom that did not match the documented record. A judge has the authority to stop a trial in which the evidence and procedures collapse. Wilters did not.

What followed is revealing.

Wilters later became the Baldwin County District Attorney, placing him in command of the very office that once stood before him as prosecutor. During Murray Jr's postconviction phase, it was Wilters who approved assigning Assistant District Attorney Kristi Hagood from the child support division, a lawyer with no criminal experience, to handle the State's response to Rule 32. Her filing was superficial and incomplete, and Wilters accepted it without requiring clarification or correction.

Hagood is now running for a judgeship in 2026.

This raises a question the system never answers.

How can a meaningful postconviction review occur when the individual now responsible for defending the conviction once presided over the trial that produced it. How does a system claim neutrality when it places the responsibility for scrutiny inside the same hands that allowed the failures in the first place.

There is no automatic requirement in Alabama that a district attorney recuse himself from a case he once oversaw as a judge. The absence of a rule does not erase the conflict. It exposes a structural flaw that makes accountability dependent on self-examination.

Beside Wilters in influence stands Hoss Mack, who served as Chief Deputy during the investigation into Brandon Hastings's death. The narrative that led to Murray Jr's arrest and conviction was built inside the command structure Mack oversaw. He later became Sheriff of Baldwin County, holding the office for seventeen years, during which his authority and political capital expanded.

Today Mack serves as Executive Director of the Alabama Sheriffs Association, shaping statewide policing priorities. Trusted sources have said he is positioned for a potential leadership role inside the Alabama Law Enforcement Agency, the state body responsible for investigating officer involved deaths.

Directly under Mack during the original investigation was Anthony Lowery, now the current Sheriff of Baldwin County. Lowery was part of the investigative chain that sustained the theory used to prosecute Murray Jr. He did not question the contradictions in the evidence or the absence of an Alabama autopsy. He did not challenge the coerced statements or the shifting witness accounts.

When Mack retired, Lowery inherited custody of the original investigative files, the evidence storage, and the institutional authority that determines whether a wrongful conviction is ever reexamined. He is now preparing to run for a full term in 2026.

The final figure in this chain is John David Whetstone, the district attorney who prosecuted Murray Jr's case. He directed a prosecution that ignored the Mississippi autopsy, relied on coerced statements, and presented a theory with no forensic foundation. He remained in office for years after the contradictions in his case were undeniable.

Taken together, these four men form a continuous chain of influence that stretches from the original investigation to the present.

A judge who became the district attorney.
A chief deputy who became sheriff, then a statewide policy voice.
An investigator who became sheriff and custodian of the evidence.
A prosecutor who retained power long after the truth should have ended the case.

The public sees titles and elections. What it does not see is the continuity of power.

The same network that built the case against Murray Jr still holds authority in Baldwin County and across Alabama. Their continued presence explains why scrutiny has been resisted and why postconviction review collapsed.

Until the power structure that created this injustice is named plainly and examined honestly, the system cannot claim to correct its own mistakes.

26 THE DEADLINE WE WERE FORCED TO FACE ALONE

When the firm stepped away, there was no transition. No handoff. No guidance. No accounting of what had been done or what had been left undone. What remained was a rapidly closing calendar and the realization that if anything further was going to be filed, it would have to be done without counsel.

This was not an abstract failure. It was immediate, concrete, and dangerous.

Advocates were not overwhelmed by theory. They were overwhelmed by time. The question was no longer what should have happened. It was what could still be done before the door closed permanently. With no legal training and no institutional support, responsibility shifted entirely onto those who had been working outside the system to support the case.

Research began immediately. Not into the facts, which were already known, documented, and organized, but into procedure. What remedies remained. Which deadlines governed. What filings were still possible. Failure would not mean another denial. It would mean the end of review.

Two federal filings stood between Murray Lawrence Jr and permanent procedural closure, a petition for certiorari to the United States Supreme Court, the final step for challenging the state court process at the federal level, and a federal habeas corpus petition, the last opportunity for a federal court to review constitutional violations after all state remedies are exhausted.

During this period, Murray Jr had no access to court dockets, no ability to monitor deadlines, and no way to know what actions were being taken on his behalf. From inside prison, he was wholly dependent on others to preserve his rights. The stakes were absolute. Missed deadlines meant silence forever.

It was during this emergency effort to understand what came next that advocates discovered something they had never been told.

The petition for certiorari filed on 04 slash 18 slash 2025 in the Alabama Supreme Court, signed by Leroy Maxwell Jr and Gabrielle Humber, contained an attorney verification stating that the statement of facts was a verbatim copy of the proposed facts listed in the application for rehearing to the Alabama Court of Criminal Appeals.

That verification was not boilerplate. It was an admission.

It meant the filing was not a strengthened presentation at the highest state level. It was not an escalation. It was not a correction of error. It was a duplication of what had already failed.

More troubling still, it did not include the counterarguments advocates had prepared in direct response to the State's Rule 32 filing. It did not incorporate the timeline corrections, factual rebuttals, credibility challenges, or forensic contradictions that had been delivered to counsel in organized, citation based form.

This was not the first time this had happened.

The same omission had already occurred at the Rule 32 stage. After the State filed its response, volunteer advocates prepared detailed counterarguments addressing factual misstatements, timeline errors, omitted admissions, witness coercion, and forensic contradictions. That work was provided to counsel with the clear expectation that it would be filed as a rebuttal.

It was never filed.

Now, at the Alabama Supreme Court level, the pattern repeated.

The certiorari petition did not state that it adopted supplemental materials. It did not reference outside rebuttal memoranda. It did not claim to incorporate additional analysis developed after the Rule 32 response. It declared plainly that the statement of facts was copied word for word from the prior rehearing application.

In practical terms, this meant the Alabama Supreme Court never saw the strongest challenges to the State's narrative, just as the Rule 32 court never had.

This was not a strategic choice explained to the family. It was not disclosed. It was not discussed. Advocates learned the truth only because abandonment forced them to read every filing themselves, line by line, with no one left to rely on.

From that moment forward, the task was no longer advocacy. It was damage control. The goal became preventing procedural default from erasing the case entirely.

While advocates scrambled to understand procedure and deadlines, Murray Jr waited. He did not know what had been filed, what had been omitted, or how close the case was to permanent closure. During this critical period, he was entirely reliant on others to preserve his rights.

Proceeding pro se was not a choice. It was not a tactic. It was the only way forward.

.

27 THE RACE AGAINST THE CLOCK

Preparing the federal habeas petition became its own investigation. The facts were already known. What was broken was the path the case had taken to reach federal court. Volunteers reconstructed the procedural history by hand, starting with the earliest Mississippi records and tracing forward through abandoned appeals, incomplete filings, and years of representation that ended without continuity. Before the case could be argued, the record itself had to be rebuilt, because state remedies were exhausted and federal court was the only remaining path.

They gathered everything the courts had scattered. Trial transcripts. Police reports. Mississippi forensic records. Docket sheets and orders from every level of review. Correspondence from prior attorneys. Timelines they had created themselves when no one else would. Only after the record was reassembled could the petition be written in a way that matched the reality it relied on.

The habeas petition was structured to force clarity. Constitutional violations were set out one by one, tied to controlling law and anchored in evidence the jury never had. Brady and Kyles governed the suppression claims. Alibi support had been withheld. Phone and cell tower evidence tied to the critical window was never disclosed. Forensic material contradicted the State's theory and was minimized or buried.

Prosecutorial misconduct followed. Under Napue and Giglio, the State cannot rely on testimony it knows is false or misleading. Jarius's credibility was the case itself. Threats, plea leverage, and minimized deals shaped the accusation. The jury was never given a complete picture of how that testimony was secured.

Ineffective assistance of counsel was presented as a sequence of failures with consequences, governed by Strickland. Alibi witnesses were not fully investigated. Phone evidence was not presented with force. Forensic contradictions were left standing. Improper argument went unchallenged. The petition tied deficient performance to prejudice and showed a reasonable probability that competent representation would have produced a different result.

Structural failures followed. Jury selection reflected bias under Batson. Juror exposure raised Remmer concerns. A conviction resting solely on testimony triggered due process scrutiny under Jackson. Actual innocence stood over all of it, not as rhetoric but as law, opening the door under Schlup and McQuiggin when procedure tried to close it.

To make the record unavoidable, the petition was organized through exhibits, each written to prove a specific point rather than overwhelm the court. This was not about tone. It was about precision. If the court chose not to engage, it would not be because the record was unclear.

Execution and mailing became their own ordeal.

The completed filings were mailed to Murray Jr at Holman Correctional Facility for review and signature, with prepaid priority envelopes so the prison could mail them on his behalf. Under federal law, the date an incarcerated person signs a filing constitutes the execution date.

That process did not proceed normally.

Prison staff did not deliver the documents to Murray Jr. They stalled inside the facility. When advocates called to ask why, they were told the prison would not release legal paperwork to an inmate unless the inmate had an attorney of record. Murray Jr did not have counsel.

The obstruction deepened when prison staff refused to allow the documents to be mailed through the prison at all. Even with prepaid envelopes included, staff stated the mail could not be processed. By denying Murray Jr access to the filings and refusing to transmit his signed documents, the prison created barriers that made compliance with federal deadlines nearly impossible.

There was no legal basis for this. Murray Jr had the right to execute and mail his own pleadings. Conditioning access on attorney involvement when he had none amounted to a denial of access to the courts.

With deadlines collapsing, advocates were forced to find attorneys who were personal friends simply to gain entry to the facility. These attorneys did not represent Murray Jr. They did not review the case. They did not file appearances. Their presence served no legal function beyond satisfying Holman's arbitrary demand so Murray Jr could sign his own paperwork.

These were not inconveniences. They were systemic barriers imposed at the most critical moment.

Several months later, the petition for certiorari was returned as incomplete for the first time. The notice identified correctable defects and allowed resubmission. Advocates corrected the filing as instructed, again navigating the same access barriers, and returned the amended petition. That corrected version was finalized and mailed on 11 slash 23 slash 2025, two days before the sixty day deadline expired.

It was returned again.

The second return was not based on substance or claims. It concerned a single technical omission on the cover page. One line of required formatting language was missing. Nothing else changed.

As the habeas deadline approached, time disappeared. Volunteers made multiple trips to Holman with two different attorney friends.

So much time had been consumed by manufactured roadblocks that there was no margin left.

When the signed paperwork was finally obtained, they got in the car and drove to Mobile.

They hand delivered the habeas petition to the Southern District Court of Alabama with only hours remaining before the deadline expired.

There was a brief moment of relief when it was accepted. Even then, it was clear this was never how the process was supposed to work.

28 TAKING ACTION OUTSIDE THE COURT

Federal filings rarely succeed, even when supported by strong records and clear constitutional violations. That reality sharpened rather than slowed the work. If the case was going to move forward, Murray Jr Lawrence Jr's story would have to be visible, accessible, and impossible to dismiss.

The website became central to that effort. What had once been a functional tool during the filing sprint was rebuilt into something far more substantial. It was no longer a placeholder or a landing page. It became a repository, designed to carry the full weight of the record and allow anyone examining the case to navigate the evidence without commentary or persuasion layered on top of the facts.

With the structure in place, the volunteers returned to the transcripts and witness statements. There were a staggering number of witnesses who began one way and shifted only after repeated questioning. The changes were not random. They followed pressure, consistently and predictably.

What stood out was not only the coercion itself, but what had never followed it. No coordinated effort had ever been made to return to those witnesses once the fear surrounding the case had faded. Testimony had been challenged. Credibility had been debated. But sworn affidavits had never been pursued in any systematic way, in part because courts had never required the State to account for how those statements were obtained.

Attention turned to what would be required to do that work correctly. Many of the people questioned in 2003 had been very young at the time, some barely adults, all inexperienced and under intense pressure. The warnings they were given carried no legal weight today, if they ever had. The passage of time had changed the legal landscape entirely.

Correcting a pressured or confused statement is not a crime. The law protects it. The goal was straightforward and long overdue. To gather sworn declarations of facts from those who had been threatened, intimidated, coached, or silenced, not to relitigate credibility, but to document how the story had been shaped before it ever reached a jury.

The distinction between mistake and perjury was made clear. Being scared, uncertain, or misled as a young person does not constitute a crime. The law protects those who come forward to correct errors, particularly in wrongful conviction cases. Courts not only allow such corrections, they encourage them. Across the country, witnesses have stepped forward years later to clarify testimony without consequence.

Equally important was what this process did not do. No witness was reopening anything against themselves. No one faced retroactive charges. No one could be dragged into a new case. There was no hidden exposure, no risk waiting on the other side of honesty.

A notarized statement of facts provided further protection. It documented that each statement was voluntary, uncoerced, and limited to the truth as the witness understood it. Nothing more. Nothing less. Each affidavit would simply explain what was seen, what was known, and how earlier statements came to be shaped by fear or pressure.

The purpose was singular. These sworn statements were not about blame. They were about correcting a record that had never been allowed to stand on its own. They offered a way for voices constrained in 2003 to finally speak freely, without threat, urgency, or consequence beyond helping restore the truth.

Media outreach followed the same principle. It was not about persuasion or spectacle. It was about exposure. Federal filings can be ignored quietly. A public record cannot. Making the case accessible meant that silence was no longer an option, and that the facts could not be buried behind procedure or delay.

The direction was clear. The filings had preserved the case. The website gave it structure. The sworn statement work would give it voice.

29 WHEN AGE REMOVED INFLUENCE

The meeting on November 12, 2025 took place without ceremony. By that point, weekly gatherings had become routine, shaped by deadlines, documents, and steady forward motion. Federal filings had been preserved. What came next would not wait on the courts.

The focus that night was witnesses.

Witness testimony had always hovered at the edges of the case. Statements had shifted. Accounts had been pressured. Fear had shaped what people said and what they withheld. These issues had been referenced in filings and argued in courtrooms, but no coordinated effort had ever been made to return to those witnesses and ask them, calmly and directly, to correct the record under oath.

That work was now underway.

Family members and volunteers had already spoken with at least four individuals whose names appeared repeatedly in the record. Over time, each had said some version of the same thing. They had been young. They had been intimidated. They had been warned. And they were now willing to tell the truth.

This was not speculative outreach. These were not cold calls. These were people who had lived with what they said for years and wanted the opportunity to clarify how their statements came to be shaped.

Affidavits were drafted with care. The purpose was not to relitigate credibility or assign blame. It was to document pressure, context, and omission. Each would be sworn, limited, and precise, focused only on what the witness knew and how earlier statements were influenced.

This kind of work had never been undertaken in Murray Lawrence Jr's case. Prior attorneys had argued coercion, but no one had systematically gathered sworn testimony to support it. What had long been discussed in theory was finally being done in practice.

The plan was direct. As sworn statements were completed, they would be submitted as supplemental exhibits to the federal habeas petition. Not as narrative. Not as advocacy. As evidence.

At the same time, completing the website was essential. It did not merely organize the record. It presented the case in full. A front-page summary. An outline of the system that failed Murray Jr, political power, defense failures, and institutional collapse. A section devoted to proof of innocence, including the full file of the confessed killer, a reconstructed timeline of the murder, the Mississippi autopsy, and detailed documentation of coerced witnesses. Every court filing. The complete trial transcript. The limited media coverage that had existed, preserved and linked, alongside a press release and clear contact information.

For the first time, anyone willing to look closely could understand the case without rebuilding it themselves. Journalists, podcasters, legal organizations, and independent reviewers could examine the full record in one place and reach out directly.

The website did not argue the case. It made the truth accessible.

The meeting ended with assignments and quiet resolve. Witness outreach would take patience and care. But the work was no longer hidden, fragmented, or confined to filings few people ever saw.

The filings had preserved the case.
The website gave it structure.
The affidavit work would put the truth on record.

30 THE MISSING CONFESSION RECORD

This was not something discovered early in the case. It did not emerge during trial, on appeal, or even during the first rounds of postconviction review. It surfaced only years later, after the record was reconstructed piece by piece and requests were made for materials that had never been questioned because their existence had always been assumed.

By the time Murray Jr was tried for capital murder, one fact was treated as settled. Jarius had admitted to killing Brandon Hastings. That admission appears in the trial transcript. It is referenced by witnesses. It is accepted by the prosecution as true. The case proceeds as though the confession exists and requires no further examination.

Only later, when the investigative record itself was requested, did the problem become visible. The confession could not be found.

There was no audio recording of a custodial interview in which Jarius admitted to the killing, no video, no written or typed statement bearing his signature, and no supplemental report memorializing the substance of such an admission. Nothing in the file described when the confession occurred, where it took place, who was present, or how it was documented. When the clerk was asked for the statement that should have anchored this part of the case, the response was brief and unmistakable. It is missing.

This was not a dispute over wording, format, or labeling. It was an absence in the record itself.

In a homicide investigation, when a suspect admits to killing the victim and that admission is relied upon by the State, some form of confession record must be preserved. The law does not require a single method. A confession may be recorded, reduced to writing, summarized in an officer's report, or incorporated into court proceedings. What matters is that it is fixed into the record in a way that allows later review. A confession cannot exist only as an assumption carried forward without documentation.

Here, the admission attributed to Jarius was not incidental. It explained the direction of the investigation, justified charging decisions, and underpinned the State's theory at trial. Yet no preserved confession record exists anywhere in the investigative file.

That absence is made more striking by how the prosecution handled the confession in the courtroom. It was referenced, but never examined in detail. No recording was played. No written statement was introduced. The jury was never walked through the circumstances of the admission or asked to consider its contents. Instead, the confession was treated as background fact, something to be accepted without scrutiny, while the focus shifted to a narrative that required Murray Jr's involvement.

That choice was not neutral. A full and detailed confession by Jarius would have fixed the timeline early, clarified whether anyone else was named, and highlighted the absence of physical evidence tying Murray Jr to the killing. It would have forced the jury to reconcile a one-person act with a two-person theory. The State relied on the existence of the confession but could not afford for its substance to be examined.

The problem does not stop with the missing confession record.

Jarius's own case did not resolve informally. His prosecution proceeded through judicial resolution by bench trial. A bench trial is not casual or symbolic. It requires a factual basis. Judges do not adjudicate guilt without some articulation of what the defendant admitted or what facts the court accepted as true. When a defendant has admitted responsibility for a homicide and is sentenced to life with the possibility of parole, that factual basis ordinarily appears somewhere in the record.

Here, it does not.

No bench trial transcript has ever been produced. There are no written findings, no stipulation of facts, and no order explaining how the court determined Jarius's culpability. Nothing in the record shows whether the court accepted a theory that he acted alone or how that conclusion was reached.

That absence intersects directly with Murray Jr's case. If Jarius was adjudicated guilty based on acting alone, that record would have undermined the State's theory against Murray Jr at its foundation. If the bench trial proceeded on a narrower or different factual basis, that too would have been material. Either way, the record should exist.

It does not.

This leads to an unavoidable question. Why did the defense not request or obtain the bench trial record of the admitted killer. There is no indication in the file that it was ever sought, produced, or reviewed. Whether this reflects ineffective assistance, lack of disclosure, or a system in which critical records were difficult to locate cannot be determined from what remains. What can be said is that the absence deprived the defense and every reviewing court of the ability to test the State's narrative against the adjudication of the person who actually killed Brandon Hastings.

Efforts to locate these missing records have revealed another layer of failure. There is no single repository that can account for what happened. The clerk does not have the confession record. The investigative file does not contain it. The postconviction record does not reference it. No custodian of records can produce either a preserved confession record or a bench trial factual basis. The story exists everywhere in testimony and assumption. The documentation exists nowhere.

Years later, advocates contacted the Alabama Board of Pardons and Paroles to request that they be added as contacts for any future parole hearings involving Jarius. It was during that call that they were informed Jarius had already had a parole hearing in 2024.

No one associated with Murray Jr had been notified. Murray Jr had not been informed. His family had not been informed. The contact list did not include them. The hearing had already occurred.

The omission extended further. Brandon Hastings's family had not been notified of the 2024 hearing.

Jarius was denied parole and informed he would not be eligible again for five years.

The issue is not the denial. It is that a parole hearing for the admitted killer occurred without notice to Murray Jr, without notice to his family, and without notice to the victim's family. In a case defined by missing records, absent documentation, and withheld information, even the parole process proceeded without transparency.

This is not a minor gap. It is a structural void.

Without a preserved confession record, there is no way to know what Jarius said when he admitted to the killing, whether he named anyone else at the time, whether the firearm theory had already entered the narrative, or what pressure preceded the admission. Without a bench trial record, there is no way to know what facts the court accepted when it adjudicated his guilt.

The State proceeded as though these answers did not matter. But they do.

In a prosecution that resulted in life without parole for one man and the possibility of freedom for the admitted killer, the absence of both a preserved confession record and a bench trial factual basis is not benign. It is one more critical failure in a case already defined by missing evidence, shifting narratives, and unanswered questions.

The confession is treated as fact.
The adjudication is treated as settled.
The records that should support both are missing.

And no one has ever explained why.

31 THE MEETING THAT CHANGED EVERYTHING

The meeting on November 23, 2025 followed a rhythm that reflected consistent momentum. Federal filings were in place. Affidavits had been drafted, organized, and distributed among the advocates who would begin contacting witnesses. The work had shifted from preservation to action.

The focus that night was coordination.

Responsibilities were clarified. Timelines were confirmed. Each sworn statement had a defined purpose and a specific witness attached to it. The outreach process was underway, and it required precision and consistency.

Time was spent walking through the website.

The walkthrough was practical, not explanatory. Everyone needed to know where to find materials quickly while speaking with witnesses. Full transcripts. Timelines. The Mississippi autopsy. Prior statements. A detailed question and answer section designed to address concerns that had come up repeatedly. The site had been built so advocates could move confidently through the record without searching through separate files or notes.

The conversation briefly turned to organization within the site itself. Under the proof of innocence section, someone suggested adding jurisdiction as a labeled dropdown alongside the other categories already there. It was raised as a matter of structure, not argument, a way to keep related documents easy to locate if needed.

The note was made. The meeting concluded.

Later that night, the work continued alone.

The jurisdiction tab was added. Documents were pulled to populate it. Mississippi records first, then Alabama filings. The task was administrative, placing existing materials where they belonged so they could be accessed efficiently.

Pages were opened and reread. Documents were placed side by side. What began as organization demanded closer attention.

The work stretched late into the night.

By the time it stopped, it was no longer a question of presentation or completeness. Something essential was missing from the foundation itself. The record did not merely raise concerns. It contradicted the assumption the entire case rested on.

What had once been accepted without challenge no longer held.

32 THE TURNING POINT HIDDEN IN PLAIN SIGHT

The realization did not arrive through theory or speculation. It came through documents that had been sitting in the record for more than twenty years.

What emerged was not another defect to be added to a long list. It was a threshold failure. Jurisdiction, meaning the legal authority of a court to prosecute a case at all, is not weighed, balanced, or excused. If it never existed, the conviction is void regardless of the evidence.

For years, pieces of this prosecution were examined in isolation. Jurisdiction appeared on issue lists alongside evidentiary disputes, witness credibility, and trial error, treated as one problem among many. What set it apart was not complexity, but character. Jurisdiction is determined by the record, does not expire, and either exists or it does not. It requires only that the record support the State's authority to prosecute, a question that had never been examined on its own terms.

Every custodial and forensic act in this case was performed by Mississippi authorities, from recovery through certification. Brandon Hastings's body was recovered in Mississippi. The autopsy was conducted in Mississippi. The cause and manner of death were certified by Mississippi. The only transfer of the remains to Alabama occurred for funeral services, not for investigation, examination, or medical review. That transfer conferred no jurisdictional authority.

The indictment alleged Baldwin County. Proof never followed.

The trial court never required it.
The prosecution never produced it.
The defense never challenged it.

Venue was never reached because jurisdiction was never established. A homicide rooted entirely in Mississippi was tried as an Alabama case through assumption alone.

Every lawful pathway by which Alabama could have exercised jurisdiction was examined against the record. Border doctrines require proof the fatal act occurred in the prosecuting state. Continuing offense theories require documented lethal conduct beginning there. Constructive presence requires an act committed in state that directly caused death elsewhere, supported by medical causation. Conspiracy requires proof of an agreement and an overt act tied to the killing. Statutory expansion still requires constitutional proof of authority.

This record satisfies none of them.

What the Indictment Required but Never Delivered

An indictment is not a narrative document. It is a jurisdictional instrument. Its function is not to tell a story, but to invoke the State's authority to prosecute by alleging facts that place the offense within that authority.

This indictment did not do that.

It alleged Baldwin County as the place of prosecution, but it did not allege facts establishing that Alabama had jurisdiction over the homicide itself. It did not allege that the fatal act occurred in Alabama. It did not allege conduct beginning in Alabama that caused death elsewhere. It did not allege a continuing offense spanning state lines. It did not allege a conspiracy with an overt act in Alabama tied to the killing. It did not allege any jurisdictional theory recognized under Alabama law.

Those were foundational omissions.

When an indictment charges a homicide, jurisdiction is not presumed from geography alone. The charging instrument must allege facts that, if proven, would authorize the State to act. Here, the indictment named a county but supplied no jurisdictional substance to support that choice.

That failure mattered because the record affirmatively contradicted the assumption embedded in the charge.

Every custodial and forensic fact placed the death in Mississippi. Alabama did not conduct an autopsy. Alabama did not establish a crime scene. Alabama did not recover forensic evidence tying the death to its territory.

An indictment that alleged jurisdiction without factual support required scrutiny. It required proof. It required the court to ask how Alabama had authority to prosecute a homicide rooted entirely in another state.

None of that happened.

The indictment was accepted without examination. The court never required the State to reconcile its charge with the forensic record. The defense never challenged the pleading. Jurisdiction was treated as a given.

What the indictment required was a factual bridge between Mississippi death and Alabama authority.

What it delivered was assumption.

That assumption was never tested. Never litigated. Never adjudicated.

Because jurisdiction is not waivable, not discretionary, and not subject to harmless error, the failure of the indictment to establish it was not a procedural flaw. It was a void at the foundation of the case.

The Moment Jurisdiction Was Abandoned

What followed showed this was not an oversight. It was substitution.

During custodial interrogation, Jarius eventually offered a location in Alabama where he claimed the murder occurred. Investigators followed him there. Nothing was found. No body. No blood. No physical evidence of any kind.

The only evidence placing the fatal act in Alabama was the statement of the admitted killer after he had been charged, threatened with capital punishment, and repositioned as an accomplice. No physical evidence corroborated that location. No forensic finding supported it. No independent witness confirmed it.

Under Alabama law, accomplice testimony cannot sustain a conviction without corroboration tending to connect the accused to the commission of the offense. Even setting aside statutory corroboration requirements, constitutional due process still requires sufficient evidence to establish every element of the crime, including territorial jurisdiction. An uncorroborated assertion contradicted by the only forensic record in the case cannot satisfy that burden. If such testimony cannot independently sustain a conviction, it cannot independently establish the State's authority to prosecute.

When a suspect provides a location and it collapses under scrutiny, the law requires the theory to collapse with it. Instead, the absence of evidence was absorbed, and the case moved forward as though jurisdiction had been established simply because it had been asserted.

During closing argument, District Attorney John David Whetstone told the jury that the State was required to prove where the crime occurred.

"You have to decide where this crime happened," he said.

He then proceeded as if it already had.

"This murder happened in Baldwin County," he told the jury.

He cited no evidence. He referenced no testimony. He pointed to no document. Jurisdiction was declared, not proven.

Judge Robert Wilters approved the exhumation of Brandon Hastings's body knowing it produced no finding inconsistent with Mississippi's autopsy. Alabama gained no proof of a gunshot, no Alabama crime scene, and no forensic basis for an Alabama homicide. Nothing from reopening the body altered cause or manner of death, and nothing from that process was provided to the defense.

The court nevertheless allowed the case to proceed as if jurisdiction had been strengthened.

Mississippi controlled the scene and the remains. Custody never transferred for investigation, only for funeral services. That transfer conferred no authority and resolved nothing.

At that point, the question became unavoidable.

Acknowledging Mississippi jurisdiction would have carried consequences the State never confronted. It would have required accepting Jarius's original confession and ending the case. It would have required relinquishing control and turning the prosecution over to another state.

The record supplies only the effect.

A confessed killer was insulated, his account reshaped, and the case redirected around him.

The Question That Was Raised and Set Aside

How did Murray Lawrence Jr's original defense attorney never raise this.

Jurisdiction and venue are threshold obligations. They are not advanced legal strategies.

Counsel possessed the Mississippi autopsy. He had recovery documents and death certificates establishing Mississippi custody at every stage. Yet he never filed a challenge. Never raised an objection. Never questioned an indictment alleging an Alabama homicide despite Mississippi forensic proof to the contrary.

The issue itself had been identified years earlier.

Before outside advocates began working on this case, a handwritten Rule 32.1(b) petition prepared by a jailhouse attorney identified the jurisdiction defect. Rule 32.1(b) provides the mechanism for challenging a conviction as void when the trial court never had jurisdiction to enter judgment.

That handwritten petition was later typed to make it readable and usable for counsel. The typed version, along with accompanying analysis and organized supporting materials, was provided to postconviction counsel at the Maxwell Tillman firm before the firm was retained.

The jurisdiction argument was not hidden or speculative. It was delivered by volunteer advocates as part of a broader list of issues and filings the firm had been asked to pursue. At the time, the jurisdiction claim was presented alongside other postconviction concerns, without full appreciation of how categorically different it was from the rest.

The firm dismissed the request to pursue Rule 32.1(b). Counsel stated that the jurisdiction petition originated with a jailhouse attorney and declined to use it.

Jurisdiction was raised again. At that point, counsel responded that the advocates were being too aggressive. After that response, the issue was not raised again.

The Rule 32.1(b) petition was never filed.

Because the filing was never made, no court ever had access to the handwritten or typed jurisdiction petition. No judge was asked to rule on the State's authority to prosecute. The jurisdiction defect remained outside the courtroom.

Every attorney who touched the case had access to the same underlying record. Courts reviewing the case had the same transcripts, the same autopsy, and the same custody documents. No judge, no prosecutor, no defense attorney, and no postconviction lawyer ever required the State to prove jurisdiction.

This distinction matters.

Jurisdiction is different.

Rule 32.1(b) exists for this exact defect. Jurisdictional failures do not expire. They arise directly from the record.

This issue had never been adjudicated.
It had never been placed before a judge.
It had never been decided.

The documents had not changed. The difference was that they were finally read together, without assumption.

Alabama never proved the death occurred in Alabama. Alabama never had jurisdiction.

A court without jurisdiction cannot convict.

The conviction is void.

33 ZERO CONSEQUENCES

If Murray Jr is released, no one will be held accountable for what happened to him.

Not the investigators who coerced witnesses.
Not the prosecutors who pursued a case without jurisdiction.
Not the court that allowed the issue to go unexamined.
Not the prison officials who blocked access to the courts when deadlines were closing.
And not the attorneys whose failures made the conviction possible.

Under Alabama law, release does not trigger accountability. It ends the case.

There is no automatic inquiry when a conviction is overturned or voided. No mandatory referral to disciplinary authorities. No requirement that a court examine how a case reached trial without jurisdiction. Once the conviction falls, the system moves on. The people who caused the harm remain insulated.

That absence of consequence is structural.

The single most consequential failure in Murray Jr's case was his original defense attorney, Willie E Huntley. Had any competent defense attorney been involved, jurisdiction would have been raised and the case would have ended. Instead, it proceeded unchecked.

Huntley possessed the Mississippi autopsy and recovery documents establishing Mississippi custody of the body. He had records showing every custodial and forensic act occurred in Mississippi. Jurisdiction was not a tactical decision left to professional judgment. It was a threshold obligation. He never raised it.

Beyond jurisdiction, Huntley failed at every stage where a defense is required to function. He did not call available witnesses. He did not present a coherent counter narrative. He did not effectively challenge the gun theory despite forensic evidence excluding a gunshot. He failed to preserve objections for appeal. He failed to interrupt a case that did not add up.

His conduct was never substantively examined by any court. No disciplinary body reviewed it. No accountability followed. A life without parole was imposed, and the attorney whose failures made that outcome possible faced no consequence.

That pattern did not end with trial counsel.

After conviction, postconviction counsel was provided with organized materials identifying the jurisdiction defect and the proper legal mechanism for raising it under Rule 32.1(b). The argument was presented in usable form. It was not pursued.

A formal grievance was later filed with the Alabama State Bar regarding Maxwell Tillman Law Group's postconviction handling of the case. The grievance did not rest on a single issue. It detailed the firm's failure to raise the jurisdictional defect despite being provided the supporting record, failure to preserve viable claims, failure to pursue available procedural remedies, and failure to protect statutory and constitutional rights during critical postconviction stages. The submission included supporting documentation, record citations, and analysis demonstrating how those omissions affected the outcome of the case.

The complaint was dismissed without findings, without hearing, and without substantive review of the underlying claims. The Bar concluded that no misconduct was warranted. A supplemental rebuttal and additional documentation have since been submitted addressing the Bar's response and expanding the record. Those materials will be posted publicly so the analysis can be evaluated independently.

That result reflects how attorney accountability functions in Alabama.

That structure extends into incarceration itself. During critical filing periods, Murray Jr's access to legal materials and outgoing mail was restricted based on internal prison directives. When clarification was requested, the explanation was simply that it was prison policy.

Not a statute.
Not a court order.
Not a written regulation publicly vetted through rulemaking.

In practice, institutional staff can announce a rule and enforce it immediately. There is no automatic review to determine whether the directive conflicts with state law or federal constitutional protections. There is no required hearing before access to legal materials is restricted. There is no independent mechanism that pauses enforcement until legality is verified.

The authority to control mail, paperwork, and movement inside a facility rests within the administrative chain of command. Yet those exercising that authority are not required to be attorneys, judges, or constitutional scholars. They are not required to demonstrate formal legal training before enforcing restrictions that affect access to the courts.

When internal directives can be created or interpreted at the institutional level and enforced without external review, constitutional rights depend on the discretion of prison administration. The burden then shifts to the incarcerated person to challenge the very system controlling his access, often while access itself is restricted.

That is how access to the courts is eroded. Not by a judge. Not by a written ruling subject to appeal. By administrative enforcement inside a prison office, where an internal directive can function as law unless and until someone successfully challenges it from within confinement.

In many states, a conviction overturned for jurisdictional failure or suppressed evidence triggers review. In Alabama, it does not. Jurisdictional failures can persist for decades without enforcement. Attorney discipline is discretionary and rare, even when the harm is severe and permanent.

Baldwin County exemplifies this structure. Allegations are raised. Complaints are filed. Nothing follows. Over time, that absence of consequence becomes institutional knowledge. Behavior is not corrected. It is carried forward.

The absence of consequence does not depend on timing. It exists regardless of when or how relief is obtained. Whether correction comes through federal review, state postconviction relief, or jurisdictional enforcement, the structure remains the same. The system is designed to resolve the case without examining how it was allowed to happen.

Courts adjudicate individual violations, not ecosystems of failure. Each breakdown is siloed. Each denial is framed as procedure. Viewed together, the pattern is unmistakable.

When a wrongful conviction is undone without consequence, the system learns that the cost of being wrong is zero.

EPILOGUE

There are countless facts proving Murray Jr's innocence. That proof exists in abundance.
But this case does not ultimately turn on innocence.

The jurisdiction violation stands apart. It does not depend on guilt or innocence at all. It voids the conviction on its face.

This case did not fail because of one mistake or one bad actor. It failed because every safeguard that should have stopped it instead aligned to protect the outcome. What makes this case exceptional is not a single error, but the stacking and coordination of failures across time, across roles, and across institutions, all moving in the same direction.

In a single prosecution, a conviction was built on a theory contradicted by the only autopsy. A homicide was pursued in a state with no forensic proof the death occurred there. Jurisdiction was never established and never substantively examined by any court. Witness coercion required coordinated participation across multiple individuals. Defense counsel failed at every stage, from investigation through trial and into postconviction review. Appellate courts declined meaningful engagement. Prison officials interfered with access to federal court.

That is not ordinary error. That is insulation from accountability.

Courts are designed to adjudicate individual violations, not ecosystems of failure. Each breakdown is siloed. Each dismissal is labeled discretion. Each denial is framed as procedure. Examined in isolation, nothing appears extraordinary. Viewed together, the pattern is unmistakable.

Murray Lawrence Jr's case touches every layer. Law enforcement. Prosecution. Defense abandonment. Judicial indifference.

Appellate silence. Postconviction obstruction. Prison interference. When every layer fails in the same direction, chance is no longer a credible explanation.

There is no doctrine that forces courts to confront systemic collapse. There is no cumulative due process rule with real force at the state level. There is no automatic trigger when jurisdiction is never adjudicated. Courts presume good faith, and the burden to disprove it is placed on the person with the least access, the least power, and the most to lose.

That is the structural failure this case exposes. And it is not isolated.

Those who have worked inside this case for years recognize the pattern because they have lived it, through direct experience with Baldwin County law enforcement, prosecutors, and courts that repeatedly closed ranks rather than correct injustice.

For decades, the focus was on proving Murray Jr's innocence. What changed everything was recognizing that innocence did not need to be argued at all when the State never had the authority to prosecute him in the first place.

That truth is no longer buried.

This story does not end here.
Not yet.

This draft was prepared to preserve the record as the work continues. What comes next will require precision, restraint, and time. This record exists so the facts cannot be erased, minimized, or ignored, and so they can be examined wherever accountability is still possible.

Justice has not yet been secured.
But it is finally within reach.

PROCEDURAL POSTURE AT PUBLICATION

As of publication in February 2026, a Rule 32.1(b) postconviction petition has not yet been filed in state court.

That decision is deliberate.

Rule 32.1(b) is the most consequential filing available in this case.. Unlike claims that turn on evidentiary disputes or trial error, a jurisdictional challenge under Rule 32.1(b) is absolute in character and unforgiving in procedure. If dismissed on procedural grounds, the claim can be permanently lost regardless of its merits.

This case now sits at the intersection of two separate but interdependent paths of review. One is state postconviction relief under Rule 32.1(b). The other is federal review, where jurisdictional defects may also be raised, but only after state remedies are properly exhausted or shown to be unavailable. A procedurally defective state filing therefore carries consequences beyond state court alone.

Recent federal filings underscored how exacting this process has become. The federal petition for writ of certiorari was returned twice for correction, including once solely to require the addition of a single sentence on a cover page. Although notice and an opportunity to cure were provided in that context, the experience demonstrated that technical enforcement is not theoretical. It is routine.

Rule 32 practice offers no comparable safeguard.

Under Alabama postconviction procedure, a Rule 32.1(b) petition may be dismissed immediately and with finality for technical defects, without leave to amend. Because jurisdictional claims are not subject to harmless error analysis and because dismissal can foreclose all further review, the margin for error is effectively zero.

For that reason, speed was not the governing consideration. Precision was.

An attorney with specific experience in jurisdictional postconviction litigation has now been retained to prepare and file the Rule 32.1(b) petition. This filing challenges the authority of the State to prosecute at all. It is not an appeal and it is not a request for reconsideration. It asserts that the judgment is void on its face and must be presented with exact compliance to every procedural requirement imposed by the state.

Nothing about this posture reflects uncertainty about the claim itself. The jurisdictional defect arises directly from the existing record. It has never been adjudicated. It does not depend on newly discovered evidence and it does not expire.

This record was assembled so that when the state postconviction filing is made, it will be insulated from avoidable procedural failure and will preserve the jurisdictional issue for review wherever accountability remains possible.

The pause is not delay.
It is protection.

The work continues.

WHAT YOU CAN DO TO HELP

If you would like to support the ongoing legal effort to obtain justice for Murray Jr., please scan the QR code below.

All donated funds are used solely for attorney fees, court filing costs, expert consultation when required by counsel, and public records requests directly related to this case.

All research, document review, prison visits, travel, website maintenance, communications, and public outreach are conducted and funded independently by unpaid volunteers. No donated funds are used to compensate volunteers in any form.

Share His Story

Donate

If you want to stay connected or offer help beyond a contribution, reach out.
We welcome anyone willing to stand with this family.

Email: JusticeForMurrayLawrenceJr@gmail.com

Website: www.justiceformurraylawrencejr.com

TIMELINE SURROUNDING THE MURDER REFERENCE

This chronology exists because no complete timeline of recorded actions surrounding the murder was ever established by investigators or presented to the jury at trial. In a capital murder case that turned on precise timing and included a documented clock change during the night in question, the absence of a coherent, tested sequence of events is not routine. It is extraordinary.

This record was reconstructed in 2023 by volunteers who assembled trial testimony, court filings, phone records, police reports, and admitted exhibits into a single chronological structure. For the first time, documented actions were placed in verified time order.

This section also serves as a detailed reference companion to Chapter 12, What the Jury Heard. Rather than overwhelm that chapter with technical sequencing, the full documented structure appears here for readers who want to examine the record in depth. It also provides a clear factual framework for any future documentary, podcast, or investigative reporting that seeks to evaluate the case against the documented timeline.

What follows reflects what the official record supports. It does not rely on narrative suggestion. It reflects only what can be anchored in the documented record when events are laid out in sequence.

APRIL 5, 2003

Evening
Brandon Hastings socializes in Baldwin County before later traveling to Foley.
Source: Trial testimony

Approximately 9:30 pm
Jarius arrives alone at Elizabeth Mixson's residence. Murray

Lawrence Jr is not present. Jarius cell phone service is disconnected, so he uses Mixson's landline to call Brandon Hastings.
Source: Trial testimony; phone records

Approximately 10:30 pm
Elizabeth Mixson goes to bed and does not observe later events that night.
Source: Trial testimony

Approximately 10:38 pm
Leon Shoots calls Brandon Hastings to make plans.
Source: Phone records; testimony

Approximately 10:47 pm
Brandon Hastings returns Leon Shoots's call.
Source: Phone records

Between 11:00 pm and 11:30 pm
Brandon Hastings, Leon Shoots, and Phillip ride to the beach in Brandon's Acura.
Source: Trial testimony

APRIL 6, 2003

Approximately 12:00 midnight
Brandon Hastings drops Leon Shoots off at Bebo's BP Car Wash in Foley.
Source: Trial testimony

Approximately midnight
Murray Jr Lawrence Jr borrows Michael Dosier's vehicle, travels briefly to Mobile, and returns. No evidence places him with Jarius or Brandon Hastings during this time.
Source: Trial testimony

Approximately 12:30 am
Leon Shoots calls Brandon Hastings regarding speakers that had been sold long before. Brandon states he is back at the beach with Jarius.
Source: Trial testimony

Approximately 1:20 am
A payphone call is placed near the Pick n Pay on County Road 49. Records attribute the call to Jarius.
Source: Phone records; testimony

Approximately 1:30 am
Debra Fudge sees Brandon Hastings alive at Bebo's BP Car Wash in Foley, seated in the driver's seat of his Acura with Jarius in the passenger seat. She later identifies Jarius in a police lineup. She is not called to testify at trial.
Source: Trial transcript

Approximately 2:00 am
Stacy Giambrone leaves Tonya Mixon's home and testifies Murray Jr was there at the time.

Between 2:00 am and 3:00 am
Daylight Saving Time change occurs, shifting clocks forward one hour. No effort is made by investigators or counsel to reconcile timelines across the time change.
Source: Time standard; record omission

Approximately 3:30 am CDT
Jarius arrives at Tonya Mixson's residence driving Brandon Hastings's Acura. Tonya Mixson and Murray Jr awaken. The speakers removed from the Acura are already on the porch.
Source: Trial testimony

Approximately 3:35 am CDT
Jarius leaves. Murray Jr and Tonya Mixson return to bed.
Source: Trial testimony

Approximately 4:30 am to 4:45 am CDT
John Wayne Mixson and Crystal Curtis Lindsey arrive seeking cocaine. Murray Jr and Tonya Mixson awaken again.
Source: Trial testimony

Approximately 5:01 am CDT
John Wayne Mixson and Crystal Curtis Lindsey are stopped by police in Fairhope. This stop establishes a fixed timestamp placing Murray Jr in Fairhope during the early morning hours. The officer who conducted the stop does not testify.
Source: Police records

Early morning before sunrise
Jarius arrives alone at Cynthia Weston's residence in Daphne, AL. He washes up and sits in the dark. Murray Jr is not present.
Source: Trial testimony

Approximate late morning to early afternoon CDT
Jarius contacts Damien Heard regarding Brandon Hastings's Acura. The vehicle is later stripped. Heard's fingerprints are recovered from the car.
Source: Trial testimony; forensic evidence

Approximately 8:30 pm to 10:00 pm CDT
Jarius contacts Murray Jr and asks for a ride. This call occurs the night after the homicide, not the night of the killing.
Source: Trial testimony

Approximately 9:00 pm to 10:30 pm CDT
Tiffany and Charles Henn observe Murray Jr briefly arrive at their residence, speak with Jarius, and leave with him. The interaction is

calm and lasts only moments. No argument, distress, or violence is observed.
Source: Trial testimony

INDEX OF PEOPLE

Alphabetize by Last Name

Akins, Mike: Fairhope Police Department sergeant involved in early steps after Brandon was reported missing.

Broadus, Vickie: Jackson County coroner who certified the cause of death as ligature strangulation based on the Mississippi autopsy.

Curtis Lindsey, Crystal: Witness who accompanied John Wayne Mixson the night of April five and faced repeated pressure in her interviews.

Dozier, Michael: Friend of Murray Jr who confirmed portions of the April five timeline including the drug run and Murray Jr's return to Tonya's home.

Fuqua, Tony: Foley officer who attended the Mississippi autopsy and noted inconsistencies between Mississippi findings and Alabama's later gun theory.

Garrett, Mackie: Jarius's father, a United States Marshal and courthouse license inspector during the early period of the case, placing the family within the courthouse network.

Giambrone, Stacey: Friend present at Tonya Mixson's home on April five whose statements shifted under aggressive interrogation about the stolen speakers.

Gordon, Blaire: Friend in the social circle around Jarius and Cynthia Weston and present during events referenced in the early timeline.

Graham, Grant: Mississippi crime scene specialist who processed the recovery site and confirmed the absence of bullets or firearm evidence.

Griffis, Steve: Former lieutenant with the Fairhope Police Department who received the Steadman gun after it was voluntarily turned in by Murray Lawrence Sr prior to Murray Lawrence Jr's arrest. The firearm was surrendered to avoid misunderstanding and was unsupported by the Mississippi autopsy, which ruled out firearm injury. Later accounts reflected a shift in how the gun's origin and relevance were described, reframing it as connected to the homicide despite no blood, DNA, gunshot residue, ballistic evidence, or forensic linkage to Brandon Hastings's death. This reframing conflicted with the Mississippi autopsy and the original chain of custody and enabled Alabama's unsupported gun narrative to proceed at trial. Griffis is now retired. See also Lawrence, Murray Jr; Lawrence, Murray Sr; McGarry, Dr Paul; Whetstone, John David; Wilters, Robert Earl.

Hagood, Kristi: Assistant District Attorney assigned to respond to Murray Lawrence Jr's Rule 32 petition despite working primarily in the Child Support Division and lacking experience in homicide or postconviction litigation. Filed the State's response under the supervision of District Attorney Robert Earl Wilters, reinforcing the original prosecution narrative while failing to address jurisdiction, the Mississippi autopsy, coerced testimony, or unresolved factual contradictions. Her filing became the operative State position when no rebuttal was submitted. She is currently a judicial candidate in Baldwin County for the 2026 election cycle. See also Wilters, Robert Earl; Whetstone, John David; Lawrence, Murray Jr.**Hastings, Brandon:** Sixteen-year-old whose disappearance and death launched the investigation and whose body was found in Mississippi with autopsy findings of ligature strangulation.

Heard, Damien: Half-brother of Jarius who was involved in stripping Brandon's vehicle after the murder.

Heard, Steve: Uncle of Damien who acknowledged receiving Brandon's toolbox and was approached by Jarius while attempting to sell the Steadman gun.

Henn, Charles: Witness who observed Murray Jr briefly arrive with Jarius the night after the homicide and leave with him. No argument, distress, or violence was observed.

Henn, Tiffany: Witness present with Charles Henn who corroborated the calm and brief interaction between Murray Jr and Jarius the night after the homicide.

Humber, Gabriel "Gabby": Attorney formerly with Maxwell Tillman Law Group who participated in Murray Jr's postconviction proceedings in 2025. Failed to file prepared rebuttal materials responding to the State's Rule 32 response and took no action during critical appellate deadlines. Departed the firm without notice to Murray Jr or his advocates and without transition, file transfer, or disclosure of pending deadlines. Her departure left Murray Jr without representation as federal deadlines approached. Currently practicing in Panama City, Florida. See also Maxwell Tillman Law Group.

Huntley, Wilmer "Willie" Jr: Defense attorney at Murray Jr's trial whose performance fell far below the standard expected in a homicide case. He failed to challenge the Mississippi autopsy, did not raise the jurisdiction defect, conducted no meaningful investigation, and allowed the prosecution's unsupported evidence and shifting theories to stand without objection. He instructed Murray Jr to wear headphones that prevented him from hearing his own trial and presented no coherent defense strategy. His inaction and omissions played a direct role in Murray Jr's wrongful conviction.

Langham, Renauld: Friend present during the beach outing on Brandon's final day and part of the timeline of his last known movements.

Lawrence, Murray Jr: Man wrongfully convicted for Brandon's death, known as Bubba though the story uses his formal name. Convicted without physical evidence and never allowed to testify even though Mississippi performed the only lawful autopsy and retained custody of the body.

Lawrence, Murray Sr: Father of Murray Jr who insisted the Steadman gun be turned in and remained consistent despite pressure from prosecutors and investigators.

Lovett, Dale: Fairhope detective involved in early missing person efforts and follow up investigative activity.

Lowery, Anthony: Baldwin County Chief Investigator during the Murray Lawrence Jr prosecution who worked under Sheriff Hoss Mack and played a central role in sustaining a narrative that conflicted with the Mississippi autopsy and forensic record. As part of the command structure overseeing the investigation, Lowery coordinated investigative direction with the District Attorney's Office while witness statements shifted and the gun theory was retrofitted to replace Mississippi's finding of ligature strangulation. He remained within the same chain of command throughout the prosecution and postconviction period as those defects went unexamined. In 2024, following Mack's retirement, Lowery was appointed Sheriff of Baldwin County by Governor Kay Ivey and now controls the same office that retains custody of the original case files and evidence. He is currently running for a full term as Sheriff in 2026. See also Mack, Huey Hoss; Wilters, Robert Earl; Whetstone, John David.

Mack, Huey Hoss: Chief Deputy of Baldwin County during the investigation and trial of Murray Jr and second in command at the Sheriff's Office. Oversaw investigators, approved reports, and coordinated with the District Attorney's Office as the case moved forward without jurisdiction, forensic proof, or a valid Alabama autopsy. His role coincided with the replacement of Mississippi's ligature strangulation findings with an unsupported gun narrative. The victim's body was transferred to Mack Funeral Home, owned by his family, creating an undisclosed conflict of interest during an active homicide investigation under his supervision. He later served seventeen years as Sheriff of Baldwin County and now serves as Executive Director of the Alabama Sheriffs Association, placing him in a position of statewide influence over law enforcement policy.

Maxwell, Leroy Jr: Attorney and principal of the Maxwell Tillman Law Group who assumed representation of Murray Jr during postconviction proceedings. Filed a second Rule 32 petition and a Petition for Writ of Certiorari to the Alabama Supreme Court but failed to incorporate prepared rebuttal materials responding to the State's Rule 32 response. Allowed the case to proceed on an incomplete and weakened record. Following the Alabama Supreme Court's denial of review, delayed disclosure of the ruling, provided no guidance regarding impending federal deadlines, and ultimately advised the family to seek new counsel without transition, file transfer, or protection of Murray Jr's procedural rights. His withdrawal left Murray Jr unrepresented at a critical stage as federal deadlines approached, forcing advocates to proceed pro se to prevent permanent closure of the case. See also Humber, Gabriel "Gabby"; Maxwell Tillman Law Group.

McGarry, Dr Paul: Forensic pathologist who performed the Mississippi autopsy and determined the cause of death as ligature strangulation, directly contradicting Alabama's gun theory.

McGowan, Dean: Baldwin County investigator involved in repeated interrogations of Jarius during which his statements shifted toward implicating Murray Jr.

McNeil, Jarius: Admitted sole responsibility for Brandon's death during custodial interrogation, stating that he alone caused the killing. That admission followed repeated questioning and explicit warnings that he faced the death penalty. After investigators escalated pressure and introduced the threat of capital prosecution, Jarius altered his account and implicated Murray Jr. His revised statements were inconsistent in mechanism, location, and timeline and conflicted with the Mississippi autopsy, which found death by ligature strangulation and no firearm injury. Jarius later waived his right to a jury and entered a bench trial posture consistent with acting alone, without naming an accomplice or establishing a verified crime scene. His original confession was never withdrawn in court and occurred before Murray Jr was charged. See also Hastings, Brandon; Lawrence, Murray Jr.

Mixson, Elizabeth: Resident whose landline phone was used by Jarius on April five due to disconnected cell service.

Mixson, John Wayne: Brother of Tonya who sold the Steadman gun to Jarius and later invoked the Fifth Amendment at trial.

Mixson, Tonya: Central witness connected to Murray Jr on April five who was subjected to coercive interrogations and threats of prosecution and whose pressured statements were used to build the State's timeline.

Morrison, Pam: Mother of Brandon whose presence and grief influenced the emotional climate of the courtroom.

Rader, Ricky: Jackson County deputy who responded to the recovery scenes in Mississippi and documented the handling of Brandon's remains.

Shoots, Leon: Friend of Brandon Hastings who last rode with him and communicated with him by phone during the early morning hours of April six.

Stewart, John: Baldwin County deputy who read Murray Jr his Miranda rights and attended the Mississippi autopsy.

Thomas, Windall: Police officer who conducted the 5:01 am traffic stop of John Wayne Mixson and Crystal Curtis Lindsey, creating a fixed timestamp placing Murray Lawrence Jr in Fairhope. Did not testify at trial.

Waters, Gloria: Juror whose answer during polling reflected hesitation rather than firm certainty in the verdict.

Wilters, Robert Earl: Circuit Court Judge who presided over Murray Lawrence Jr's trial and exercised gatekeeping authority over evidence, argument, and jury instruction. Allowed the prosecution to advance a firearm-based theory of homicide despite the Mississippi autopsy establishing death by ligature strangulation and documenting no gunshot wound or firearm injury. Did not require the State to reconcile its theory with the only lawful autopsy or to establish jurisdiction despite all custodial and forensic acts occurring in Mississippi. Approved proceedings that permitted implication to substitute for proof, including the introduction of a gun narrative unsupported by medical or forensic evidence. Did not intervene when jurisdiction was assumed rather than proven and did not require the State to meet its threshold burden of authority to prosecute. He now serves as District Attorney of Baldwin County. See also Whetstone, John David; McGarry, Dr Paul; Lawrence, Murray Jr.

Whetstone, John David: District Attorney who prosecuted Murray Lawrence Jr and directed the State's theory of the case from indictment through trial. Advanced and sustained a firearm-based homicide narrative despite the Mississippi autopsy conclusively establishing death by ligature strangulation and documenting no gunshot wound, projectile, or firearm injury. Framed questioning and argument to suggest medical uncertainty where none existed, relying on hypotheticals and implication rather than evidence. Continued to pursue the gun theory after the autopsy findings were known and uncontested, and after no forensic, ballistic, or crime scene evidence supported firearm involvement. Relied on witness testimony that shifted only after repeated interrogation, threats of capital punishment, or inducement, while minimizing or excluding testimony that contradicted the State's theory. Asserted Alabama jurisdiction without producing proof that the fatal act occurred in Alabama or that any recognized jurisdictional theory applied. Presented location and participation as established fact during closing argument without evidentiary support. Remained District Attorney of Baldwin County long after his involvement in Murray Lawrence Jr's prosecution. See also Wilters, Robert Earl; McGarry, Dr Paul; McNeil, Jarius; Lawrence, Murray Jr.

White, David: Foley investigator involved in early missing person work and Alabama's continuation of the investigation.

Weston, Cynthia: Former girlfriend of Jarius whose testimony helped frame the environment around his changing stories and the prosecution's theory.